D1569827

Being and Worth

Being and Worth extends recent depth-realist philosophy to the question of values. It argues that beings both in the natural and human worlds have worth in themselves, whether we recognise it or not. It defends this view through an account of the human mind as essentially concerned with what is independent of it.

The book builds on Roy Bhaskar's proof that facts can entail values, and it aims to repeat in the realm of ethics his argument that experiment and change in science show that there is a depth-dimension of real structures in nature and society. This it does by a partial defence and immanent critique of Spinoza's philosophy of mind and ethics. It argues that reason is a principle in humankind which is not human-centred, but takes us out of ourselves to value beings for what they are. This leads in the end to an ethics which owes more to St Augustine than to Spinoza, in that it rests on the idea that 'being as being is good', though not all beings are equally good. Several obvious objections to this view are answered.

Conclusions follow both for environmental ethics – that natural beings should be valued for themselves, not just for their use to us – and for justice in the human world, based on the idea that humans are unique and equal in respect of 'having a life to live'.

Andrew Collier is Reader in Philosophy at the University of Southampton. His publications include *R.D. Laing, Scientific Realism and Socialist Thought, Socialist Reasoning* and *Critical Realism*. He has published many articles in *Radical Philosophy* and is a member of the editorial collective.

Being and Worth

Andrew Collier

London and New York

First published 1999 by Routledge
11 New Fetter Lane, London EC4P 4EE

Simultaneously published in the USA and Canada
by Routledge
29 West 35th Street, New York, NY 10001

© 1999 Andrew Collier

Typeset in Garamond by Routledge
Printed and bound in Great Britain by
TJ International Ltd, Padstow, Cornwall

British Library Cataloguing in Publication Data
A catalogue record for this book is available from the British Library

Library of Congress Cataloging-in-Publication Data
A catalog record is available on request

ISBN 0–415–20735–5 (hbk)
ISBN 0–415–20736–3 (pbk)

Contents

Introduction

At one level, this book can be seen as an essay in critical realist ethics.[1] It presupposes that you *can* derive an 'ought' from an 'is', as Roy Bhaskar has argued; it is a search for an 'intransitive dimension' for morality, that is a moral reality which it is up to us to discover, rather than one which it is down to us to have invented. Bhaskar's suggestion that all ills are absences is a corollary of my main conclusion. However parts of it are so speculative and, to many minds, so strange, that I feel I should make a few preliminary remarks about what I think I am doing.

Philosophy exists because there are various beliefs each of which we have good reasons for believing, yet which contradict each other and so cannot all be true. It is therefore to be expected that philosophers will spend most of their mental energy thinking about undecided issues, following arguments the outcome of which is not known in advance, and when arrived at, is still of doubtful truth. However the conflict of sets of ideas occurs not only in individual minds, but between different ideologies in society at large. In consequence much philosophy is adversarial in nature, defending views that the philosopher thinks are true and important against those that he or she thinks are false and pernicious.

For myself, while I do spend more energy on worrying at undecided problems, when it comes to writing books the case is different. I have hitherto used them mainly to defend ideas that I am fairly certain are true: a realist theory of knowledge, a non-reductive naturalism about the social world; and politically, that capitalism will continue to rob the poor and ruin the earth so long as it exists, that politics is about class struggle and so on. This does not mean that my conclusions have not sometimes surprised me: for instance, when I started writing *Socialist Reasoning* I expected to show that bridges could be built from liberal political philosophy to socialist politics; by the time I had finished, I was convinced that of all political philosophies, liberalism had about the second least to be said for it, after fascism. But on the nature of socialist politics itself, I was in no doubt. I see no reason to be ashamed of this relative certainty: to doubt everything is not to have an open mind, for an open mind is one which is open to the possibility of being convinced by one opinion or another, and if this were not a real possibility, there would be nothing to be said for having an open mind anyway. I think there are as good reasons for regarding the case against capitalism as closed, with a verdict of 'guilty', as for believing that the sun will rise tomorrow, and that I am not a tree frog.

My practice hitherto of writing in defence of ideas about which I am fairly sure is not because of a residual Cartesian lust for certainty; it is partly justified by the polemical 'needs of the conjuncture'. But in the present book I shall be presenting ideas about which I am nothing like so convinced myself. I also suspect that they will be regarded by many others as wildly metaphysical in the bad sense – as 'looking for a black cat in a dark room in which there is no cat', as Bergson described metaphysics. Nevertheless *if* they are true, they do also have some topical importance. They tie up with the ecological concerns of many contemporaries; and at a time when a single ideology has become pervasive in the northern hemisphere, and dominant worldwide – an ideology which may be described as totalitarian commercialism – they 'bend the stick' as far as possible in the other direction. To anticipate, the central idea that I am working towards – the black cat that I am after – is the medieval doctrine that *being* and *good* are convertible terms, which I think can be expressed in modern logical parlance by saying that they have different senses but the same reference. This conclusion, when spelt out a bit, entails a recognisable position within contemporary ecological philosophy – roughly the position described by Sylvan (1985: 40–41) as intermediate between deep and shallow ecology. Two readers of an earlier manuscript have latched on to this and wondered why, on the one hand, I do not engage in detail with other recent texts in this area (several of which I have a high regard for), and on the other hand, why I spend so much time discussing Spinoza's philosophy of mind and of its place in nature. My reasons are as follows. First, this book was conceived out of a consideration, not of recent ecological debates, but of Spinoza's and Augustine's philosophy (and to a degree, that of Macmurray and Heidegger). My relative neglect of ecophilosophical texts is not a case of unacknowledged debts; neglect of Spinoza and Augustine would be. Second, a philosophical book (unlike say a political manifesto) is not primarily to be judged by its conclusions, but by its arguments. The central argument of this book is that Spinoza's metaphysics of mind was essentially correct, but that the ethical conclusions to be drawn from it are not entirely those that Spinoza in fact drew, but are closer to Augustine's theory of the worth of being. Third, the Augustinian conclusion has implications for the whole of ethics, not just for environmental ethics. To illustrate this, I have added a chapter on the worth of humankind and the nature of justice.

There is also a more general reason. A philosophical book should be relevant to the contemporary problems confronting humankind, but that does not mean that it should be relevant to contemporary philosophy, or intellectual fashions generally. It is not desirable that philosophical writing should always be engaging with contemporary thinkers, and until the sixth chapter of this book, almost all the thinkers whom I discuss at length are at least dead, if not dead some centuries. Since the thought typical of any age has the primary function of hiding the realities of that age and perpetuating its evils, it is a priori likely that the ideas of other ages will be more relevant to the problems of this age than the ideas of this age will. So I hope I need not apologise for discussing nineteenth- and early twentieth-century thinkers rather than contemporaries, and Augustine and Spinoza more than either. This does not mean that I don't think today's writers have anything worthwhile to say; apart from the fact that to defend such a view would be a 'performative contradiction' in undermining interest in my own work, both the critical realism of Roy Bhaskar, and some ecological philosophy with similar realist assumptions, have bearing on my conclusions. But these I shall discuss briefly after the main argument is concluded.

The layout of the book is as follows: in the first chapter, I defend the idea that there are values independent of humankind, using fairly informal arguments, some of which are not original and are already well known. In the next three chapters I defend a Spinozist ethic as a stepping-stone position, and try to show that it implies conclusions which Spinoza himself did not draw, about the objectivity of worth.[2] In the fourth chapter I also discuss the apparent contradiction between the position arrived at and the communitarian approach to ethics, which some of my writings have been (not unreasonably) read as defending. In the fifth chapter I look at difficulties for the position I have arrived at; and in the sixth chapter I relate my conclusions to some contemporary challenges to anthropocentricity. The idea that beings have intrinsic worth applies to human beings too, and the idea of a hierarchy of beings raises the issue of what justice for human beings should be, as one instance of that ontological justice that gives each level of being its evaluative due. The final chapter is devoted to this issue. I append an essay on the existentialist ideal of authenticity, which suggests that it is closer to my conclusions here than to the subjectivism to which it is often assimilated.

1 Are there values independent of humankind?

It is often taken for granted that it is only human beings who bring values into the world; that without us, the world would be comprised of 'brute facts', i.e. valueless facts. Though this view has been challenged by 'deep ecology', the challenge easily (though not inevitably) slips over into a kind of neo-paganism: submission to a powerful but finite deity with ends indifferent to our own. I find such views (e.g. certain versions of the 'Gaia hypothesis')[1] incredible and dangerous; I intend to argue for values existing independently of us, in terms which make no assumptions either for or against any theology, whether neo-pagan or Judaeo-Christian, though I shall refer to theological positions from time to time.

One philosopher who has rejected values independent of us in an explicit way, and has made such rejection a keystone of his thought, is Jean-Paul Sartre (in *Being and Nothingness*, 1957b). His whole conception of unconditioned, 'absurd' freedom is based on the idea that we cannot justify our choices in terms of any pre-existing values, since it is only our choices that bring values into being. But to answer 'No' to the question posed in the title of this chapter could mean either of two things. It could mean:

(I) there are values only because we have them.

This is what Sartre means. But this does not commit him to:

(II) all values have value only because they are conducive to human welfare.

That (I) and (II) are distinct can be shown by the example of cruelty to animals. If, as Sartre holds, we choose our values, then we *may* choose to condemn cruelty to animals, and to condemn it, not for the sake of some ulterior human good (e.g. because cruelty corrupts its agent), but purely for the sake of the animals. And in general, though the reasons for this are not worked out theoretically, Sartre prefers an action whose motive does not refer back to the agent, to one whose motive does. In *The Transcendence of the Ego* (1957a: 56), he gives the following example:

I pity Peter, and I go to his assistance. For my consciousness only one thing exists at that moment: Peter-having-to-be-helped. This quality of 'having-to-be-helped' lies in Peter. It acts on me like a force. Aristotle said it: the desirable is that which moves the desiring.

Sartre takes up cudgels against the egoistic moral psychology of La Rochefoucauld (in the English context, Hobbes would be a more familiar example), which analyses pity as an unpleasant feeling occasioned by the other's suffering, which feeling, since it is unpleasant, motivates action which will remove it. Sartre rightly points out that pity does not aim to remove *itself as a feeling*, but to remove the suffering of the other. Sartre thinks that all unreflective desires are like this. In reflective desires, on the other hand, 'It is no longer Peter who attracts me, it is *my* helpful consciousness which appears to me as having to be perpetuated' (1957a: 59). The original desire to help Peter has, as Sartre puts it, been 'poisoned'; and this is so whether the reflective desire takes an egoistic or a moral form (for example, one might help Peter in the hope of getting one's photo in the local paper, or in order to become a more virtuous person; both are 'poisoned' in that they refer back to oneself, rather than having no end beyond Peter's being helped).

I have three things to say about this argument: (1) the word 'reflective' may cause confusion. If the contrast were between desires involving thought and desires acted on without thought, Sartre's judgement would be misplaced. Thoughtful action need not be self-referential, and spontaneous action can be: consider a surgeon coping with a highly complicated emergency, and on the other hand, a media 'personality' responding 'instinctively', as we say, in the way that will show themselves off in the best light. It is reflection only in the sense of self-reference that poisons desire.

(2) In Sartre's example, the helping act is not done for the benefit of the agent, but it *is* done for the benefit of a human being, namely Peter. Such cases will certainly have the central place in a moral theory. But with regard to the point at issue, this is an accidental feature of the case. The contrast is not between self-regarding and other-regarding desires, but between desires that involve a reference to the desirer, and those that don't. Hence it could just as well have been the-cat-having-to-be-rescued, a-species-having-to-survive, or a-landscape-having-to-be-protected.

(3) So far so good – but now I must part company with Sartre, since he thinks that values, though they appear to us as in the object, exist only because of us – and 'us' considered as individuals, not as a species. They are *in* the object, but *for* the subject. To Peter's enemies, he does not appear as having-to-be-helped. If we want to argue for non-arbitrary, objective values, we have to address ourselves to issue (I).

Are there values, then, only because we have them? It all depends what you mean by values. But this does not mean that the concept of value is up for arbitrary definition; rather that there are degrees of value-likeness: there are in the world a gradation of value-like features, so that one could draw the line at any of a number of places and say 'this side there are values, that side there are not', with some plausibility. Values in the strongest sense seem to exist only for us; *moral* values, for instance. It may be wrong for us to hunt foxes, but it is certainly not wrong for foxes to hunt geese. Certain kinds of concern for our own future seem to be unique to human beings, too. But we cannot deny that at least the higher animals are conscious, and experience pleasure and pain and fear and frustration – and these experiences are also an essential part of our value-having. Even lower organisms have needs and active tendencies to fulfil them. These features are also essential parts of what it is for us to have values; so we may say that all living organisms share more or less (some more, some less) of our nature as beings that value. It seems arbitrary to draw the cut off point at any given place on this scale of complexity of living organisms; better to recognise that it *is* a scale – that having values is not an all-or-nothing thing, but a matter of degree. And once that is granted, I see no reason to set *any* lower limit to this scale; in so far as even, say, an outcrop of rock possesses a 'tendency to persist in its being' (what Spinoza calls a *conatus*), one can ascribe to it *some* sort of value-having, though of course it is not alive, let alone conscious, and therefore it 'has values' only in a very attenuated way. Now if anyone wants to say that these cannot count as values at all, I would not quarrel with them. It seems to me a matter of verbal convention where if anywhere on the scale of value-like properties we draw the line and say 'above here, values; below here, no values'. But it is *not* a matter of verbal convention that there is a scale. Some things share more, some less, of what it is for us to have values. Here we may apply a slogan that I have criticised in other contexts: 'God made the spectrum, we make the pigeon-holes.'

Now let us pass to the second question: do all values have value only as conducive to human welfare? On what grounds might anyone answer 'Yes' to this question? I can think of three possible grounds: (1) someone might hold that God is the arbiter of all values, and that he created the whole universe for our benefit alone. Some theologians seem to have held this, and many hostile critics allege that the whole Judaeo-Christian tradition is committed to it. The latter is surely false. According to Genesis 1, God saw that creation was good even before he created life, and again at various stages before he created us. That he gave us dominion and use of other creatures implies that human good takes some sort of priority over other goods, but not that there are none. This indicates the existence of independent goods in the first sense. Second, there are laws such as 'Thou shalt not muzzle the ox when he treadeth out the corn' (Deuteronomy 25:4), and proverbs such as 'A righteous man regardeth the life of his beast:/ But the tender mercies of the wicked are cruel' (Proverbs 12:10). This indicates the existence of independent goods in the second sense. And as to the idea of God as the arbiter of good, most reputable theologians have taken the view that 'God is good' *says* something, as it would not if 'good' just meant 'whatever God chooses'.

(2) It might be asked: what *could* values be if not things conducive to human welfare? However, I think I have already answered that, in arguing that there are values of some sort had by other creatures, independently of us. And if someone says 'Well, yes, values of a *sort*, but why should we be concerned about that sort of values?', I think the ground has shifted. Grounds are being required, not for believing that values exist, but for caring about them. This takes us to (3).

(3) It might be asked: maybe other beings have values, but what is that to us? This, I regret to say, was Spinoza's position: the world is not made for us, 'God or Nature' provides for the sharks as well as for us, and sharks' interest in eating us is as legitimate as ours in eating them – but what is their interest to us? We are beholden only to our own kind. It is a paradox to which we shall have to return that despite the obvious affinity of Spinoza with deep ecology (spelt out, for example, by Arne Naess in his article 'Spinoza and Ecology', 1977), Spinoza thought we could use animals at our own convenience, and that 'the law against killing animals is based more on empty superstition and unmanly compassion than sound reason' because 'they do not agree in nature with us' (*Ethics* II.236–237, in Spinoza 1985).

The problem about this sort of argument is to find out where it stops. If I am not beholden to sharks or pigs or orchids merely because I am not one, why should I be beholden to women or Australians or members of the Faculty of Social Science, since I am not one? If carried to its extreme, this argument leads to egoism. So we must ask whether there are any good reasons not to carry it to its extreme once we have embarked on it. But first, let us ask whether egoism is false. By 'egoism' I mean the view that the motives of all human actions refer back to the agent's wellbeing. My arguments against this view are not new, but they need to be set out here.

My claim is that egoism is *false*, that is, that we are not really egoists. Yet some have claimed to be – for example Max Stirner, who said that he only kissed away the frown from his beloved's brow because it displeased him. But *why* did it displease him, if not that he wanted her to be happy. A real egoist would have said 'the silly cow's miserable again', and gone to get a beer. Maybe he thought that improving her mood would improve his chances of a night's pleasure – but I doubt whether a real egoist would even want to make love, since the desire to give one's partner pleasure is essential to sexual desire. For an egoist, masturbation is no substitute, but the real thing. Suppose Stirner were to reply: never mind *why* my beloved's being happy would make me happy; the point is that it is only because it would that I want her to be happy – so I really am an egoist. At this point one might ask: would it do if you *thought* your beloved were happy, even though she wasn't? This question is the great divide, determining in which ocean we end up. On it turns the issue whether we regard happiness (or whatever we call the good which we seek) as a subjective state, or as an objective end, which is in some measure independent of our consciousness of it. I shall follow up the consequences of the question to their extreme conclusions. If the result seems hopelessly paradoxical, I think the paradox could be removed by finding some other word than 'happiness' for the good which we seek. But for myself, I am reluctant to surrender that word to the subjectivists.

First then, where does the subjective conception of happiness as essentially a matter of conscious feeling take us? To reiterate two well-known examples: (1) suppose we could be wired to a machine that would give us intense 'happiness' on the push of a button? Would we spend our lives button-pushing? If someone did, would we not say: poor fellow, he doesn't know what he's missing? (2)If someone is miserable because of the fate of her friends, would she take the chance of an operation that would make her forget about that fate, or cease to care about it? These examples show that we desire other things than happiness, in the subjective sense of 'happiness'. But do we in fact use the word 'happiness' in an objective sense, in which it necessarily involves things independent of the subject's consciousness?

Suppose a man's whole life has been devoted to securing his children's prosperity. They have emigrated to America, and he believes they are now millionaires. In fact, they have died in poverty there. His faithful valet keeps the news from him, and for years he lives, and in old age dies, in 'blissful ignorance'. Poor man; no one would change places with him; no one would call him happy.

My suggestion is that happiness is to do with what you (at the deepest level) want, being what happens, whether you are aware that it happens or not. It is possible to object to this usage, but at the price of ejecting the word 'happiness' from the place in our moral vocabulary that it has always enjoyed.

On this view we can make sense of that wise saying of the Greeks, 'Call no man happy until he is dead.' Perhaps more examples are necessary, to dispel the strangeness of this saying: a scientist has been working all her life to develop a cure for a horrible disease. Eventually she discovers her wonder-drug, tests it with great success, markets it, and receives letters of thanks from thousands of patients who have been pronounced cured. She dies a happy woman. Then long-term side effects emerge, more painful than the original disease. All those treated by the drug die in agony. The drug is banned, but by now it has got into the hands of unscrupulous dictators who use it as a chemical weapon. No one would call such a scientist a bad person, but she is certainly an unhappy one. Since she is also fictional, one more case.

Oliver Cromwell never lost a battle; he vanquished his enemies, military and political; he secured for his country those liberties he thought most important. He died one of the most powerful men in Europe. But ... within three years of his death, his regime had collapsed, his army dispersed, his body had been exhumed and desecrated, his closest comrades at best disgraced, at worst hanged, drawn and quartered, his laws repealed, his religion persecuted. Unhappy man. But ... within thirty or so years, the memory of his exploits had made it easy to oust a new tyrant; religious toleration and parliamentary government, for which he had fought, were permanently secured; the people and ideas he was associated with were revalued. Happy man. But ... within the next century the Whig oligarchy and their successors which inherited this parliamentary government made Mammon their god, brought parliament to a new low of corruption, and religion to a cynical worldly-wise minimum, and dispossessed the peasantry by enclosures of the sort that it had been Cromwell's earliest claim to fame to have resisted. Unhappy man. But ... 200 years on his name inspired the new movement towards reform ... But then again the legacy of his policies in Ireland is still causing injustice and, till very recently, bloodshed. Was Cromwell a happy man? I think that it is too soon to say.

If you will not follow my use of 'happiness', at least accept that what moves us, worries us, excites us, gives us courage or overcomes us with dejection, is not the prospect of our subjective experiences, but the prospect of real transformations of the wider world.

We are not egoists. But if our values do not lead us back to our own subjective interests *as individuals*, why must they lead us back to the good of our own species only? Is there any ground for saying 'What is that to us?' about other species' values, that is not also a ground for saying 'What is that to me?' about other people's values.

Spinoza's account is that I am saddened by the sadness, and gladdened by the gladness, of another being that is 'like me'. What he means is another human being. But likeness, surely, is a matter of degree. Should we not be – and are we not – moved to a lesser extent by the plight of beings less, but still somewhat, like us? I believe that if Spinoza were consistent, he would have to recognise degrees of beholdenness to all beings, since all have a *conatus*, a tendency to persist in their being – those grades closest to us having the most claim on us. This view is closer to the truth but still on shaky ground. For in the first place, we need to ask 'Like us in what respect?', otherwise we might find ourselves more beholden to fruit bats than to horses, since the former share our need for vitamin C, or indeed (as Britons) more beholden to polar bears than to Australians, because the former live in the northern hemisphere. We need some objective ordering of beings, perhaps along the lines of Spinoza's conception of more or less complex individuals, capable of correspondingly more or less interaction with the rest of nature. And once we have got this, we can dispense with the services of the concept of 'likeness'. After all, it would be ridiculous enough to argue that snails ought to be more moved by the plight of squids than by ours, since they are both molluscs. For on the one hand it is not closeness on, but height up, the scale that counts; and on the other, it is only our place at the top of the scale (i.e. as capable of more interaction with – and hence knowledge of – more of nature) which enables us to have values *simply because other beings have those values* at all. There are no Animals' Dispensaries for Sick People.

It is clear enough that when Spinoza says 'likeness' he means 'likeness with regard to rationality'. But it is, I have argued, rationality and not likeness that is crucial. And what is rationality here? For Spinoza, the tendency to correct thinking, to replacing inadequate ideas by adequate ones, and thus to transform not only our knowledge but also our emotions, since emotions are not blind impulses or feelings, but involve ideas about things. But for Spinoza, rationality must also have an equivalent description in bodily terms: the capacity to affect and be affected by more things in more ways. This comes close to Macmurray's existentialist definition of reason as 'the capacity to behave consciously in terms of the nature of what is not ourselves. ... Reason is thus our capacity for objectivity' (1935: 19) – of which more in chapter 3. Thus reason – that which marks our species off from the rest of nature – involves precisely *the capacity not to be anthropocentric*.

So it is the *same fact* – our rationality in this sense – that grounds the judgements that (a) we can be moved by the values of other beings, independently of any ulterior value they may have for us, and (b) we are higher beings, and hence our needs take priority in certain respects, not just because they are ours, but on grounds of the objective order of nature.

On this basis, we can defend (1) the existence and claim on us of values other than those conducive to the ulterior good of our species, and also (2) our right to override certain of those values for the sake of our own when this is necessary (though not wantonly); but finally we must defend (3) a conception of *our* good which *includes* the good of other beings. So if I say that there are values other than those conducive to human welfare, I am saying that we can pursue values that are independent of us for no *ulterior* good of ours, though their pursuit is a good for us; that is, these other values are not a *means* to our good, but they may become *part of* our good. The good for us can include the good of other beings because we are capable of recognising that good and furthering it for its own sake; and it belongs to our nature as beings that can interact with and know more of nature than any others can, to recognise and further these independent goods. Our highest glory is to be a species with non-self-referential aims.

This conclusion is equally alien to the subjectivism of our century, which tells us that it is only our experience of things that is important, not the things we experience; and to recent demands that we should abdicate our dominion over nature. Of historical moral philosophies, I think the one that comes closest to the truth is St Augustine's. This sounds surprising, since I have made my case without appeal to theological premises, while Augustine's whole moral philosophy rests on the propositions that God is the supremely good being and the creator of all other beings; and furthermore that the first duty, which is the necessary and sufficient condition of all others, is to love God rightly: 'Love and do what you will!' Nevertheless, if we bracket off this part of Augustine's ethics for the purposes of this argument, what might be called the sublunary sector of Augustine's ethics can be summarised as follows:

1   'Being as being is good'. Values are not just states of affairs we aim to bring about; everything that exists is, to a degree, a value, and has a corresponding claim on our love.
2   There is an objective order of beings; more perfect beings are greater goods and have a greater claim on our love. Evil comes from loving lesser goods more than greater ones.
3   Human beings are more perfect than other material beings, and hence have a greater claim on our love. Hence lesser beings may if necessary be sacrificed for human welfare. However, we may not treat any being as worthless.

This ethic requires a whole lot of metaphysical work to justify it, which I have so far only hinted at. Furthermore Augustine's hierarchy of beings includes questionable Platonist elements. For instance he gives as an example of the subordination of love of a higher being to that of a lower, a greedy person preferring gold to justice. This suggests that Augustine conceived justice to be a real entity, like a Platonic idea. And on the nuts and bolts of morality, of course, Augustine is very much a child of his time. Nevertheless, he anticipates Trotsky's formulation of the ends of socialism by some 1,500 years:

> Trotsky: 'the end is justified if it leads to increasing the power of man over nature and to the abolition of the power of man over man.'
>
> (1964: 395)

> Augustine: '[God] did not wish the rational being, made in his own image, to have dominion over any but irrational creatures, not man over man, but man over beasts.'
>
> (*City of God*: book XIX, ch. 15, p. 874)

But Augustine has the advantage over Trotsky in that he admits goods independently of us; so the question, for example, whether we allow tigers to survive cannot be, as it is for Trotsky, a matter of our subjective taste. This has far-reaching consequences for the way in which we use our dominion over nature. Trotsky is right, as against some ecologists, in recognising that the question is not whether, but how we exercise that dominion; but wrong to think we may answer that question as we please, without reference to goods outside ourselves. To do so would be to go against our own nature as rational beings, by virtue of which alone we may justify our claim to dominion.

2 Towards Spinozism
The cognitive paradigm of morality

The Combats of Good & Evil is Eating of the Tree of Knowledge. The Combats of Truth & Error is Eating of the Tree of Life

(Blake 1966: 615)

If value or goodness is an attribute of beings in themselves, ethics will presumably have to be a cognitive discipline: claims about good and evil will be true or false according to whether the beings that are said to be good or evil really are so. But to make this claim without more ado would look suspiciously like intuitionism. It needs to be shown as the conclusion of an argument; however the premiss of that argument will also be a cognitive paradigm of ethics, but one with rather more clearly 'naturalistic' credentials. In this chapter I intend to defend a Spinozistic version of the cognitive paradigm of ethics as preferable to non-naturalistic ethics. In the following two chapters I will argue that the logic of Spinozan ethics pushes us beyond Spinoza's anthropocentrism towards something closer to the theory of the good adumbrated by St Augustine.

Spinoza maintained a cognitive paradigm, not only in ethics as a philosophical discipline, but in moral life itself; he held that the best way to come to lead a morally better life is by coming to have truer ideas about life. This contrasts sharply with a paradigm of ethics which has tended to dominate moral thinking for some centuries, and is most clearly exemplified by Kant: the moralistic paradigm of ethics. This paradigm is often identified with morality as such, to the extent that rejection of it is seen as at best an excuse for immorality, at worst a prescription for amorality.

The moralistic paradigm can be sketched as follows: there is a special set of motives or imperatives which are the moral ones; they are not reducible to or instrumental towards or derivative of or explicable by any other, non-moral motives or imperatives or ends; they should always take precedence over other motives etc.; it is always possible to obey the moral rather than the non-moral injunction, and every individual is responsible to do so; not to do so is precisely what it is to be immoral; any principle or good which cannot oblige in this way is a non-moral one.

I think Kant held all these views without reservation, and most moral philosophers since Kant have worked with some such model, even when they have modified one or other aspect of it (e.g. the utilitarians do try to explain the moral in terms of non-moral ends, but once the utilitarian imperative is set up, it binds in exactly the way described here, each person being responsible to put general utility before other considerations, etc.). I also think many people take some such model for granted, without any philosophical reflection on it.

Part of the attractiveness of this moralistic paradigm, evident in Kant (and derived by him from Rousseau) is its rugged egalitarianism. Some people may lack health or wealth or culture or intelligence or beauty, it says, and there is nothing that they can do about this. But they need not despair, since these non-moral goods are worth nothing beside moral goodness, and that is something everyone who seriously tries can have. This is not egalitarianism in the political sense, and while it may appeal to the same sentiments, can form the basis of an argument that political egalitarianism is not essential, since in the crucial respect, we all have equal opportunities, i.e. to be moral.

The adherent of the moralistic paradigm sees views of ethics which urge people to act otherwise than can be prescribed in its characteristic manner, as at best occasions of immorality, at worst instances of amoralism. Yet every part of this paradigm is contentious. Arguments are not lacking to the effect that obligations are specific to certain groups, that some obligations oblige institutions not individuals, that duties can conflict and so on. But perhaps the most radical case against the paradigm is that practical adherence to it causes avoidable evils and prevents realisable goods. In the first place, because the non-moral goods that the paradigm devalues (since they cannot be pursued in the manner it calls moral) are not entirely fortuitous, and a community which accepted the moralistic paradigm might find it impossible not to neglect them shamefully. Indeed there have been such communities of moral puritans, among whom neither intelligence nor culture nor beauty nor gaiety nor the arts and sciences could flourish. Such a spiritual desert is not, I think, a *corruption* of the moralistic paradigm, but a necessary consequence of its serious pursuit.

And second, because of the well-known *moralistic paradox*, that the pursuit of morality for its own sake leads not to morality but to the vice of pharisaism; conversely it may be suggested that the way in which moral goodness is actually best achieved is as a result of the pursuit of some *other* good. Instances of this idea may be called non-moralistic paradigms of ethics. Each is an ethic in the sense that it proposes a way to achieve the best common life amongst people; but that way is not by 'being moral'. To give two instances: the political paradigm of ethics, as expressed by this passage from Plekhanov:

Put people in reasonable social relations, i.e., in conditions where the instinct of self-preservation of each of them ceases to impel him to struggle against the remainder: co-ordinate the interests of the individual man with the interests of society as a whole – and virtue will appear of its own accord, just as a stone falls to the earth of its own accord when it loses any support. Virtue requires, not to be *preached*, but to be *prepared* by the reasonable arrangement of social relations. By the light-hearted verdict of the conservatives and reactionaries of the last century, the morality of the French materialists is up to the present day considered to be an *egotistical* morality. They themselves gave a much truer definition: in their view it passed entirely into *politics*.

(1974: 490–493)

This is clear enough and has a good deal of truth in it so far as it goes, though its value is limited by the consideration that we haven't yet got such a rational society, and can live better or worse lives in the interim – and the duty of working for socialism tells us nothing at all about what we should do when we are not on the picket line or at political meetings.

A second instance is a specifically religious paradigm, associated with those who have been called 'antinomians' (usually by their opponents, though some claim the title). While often seen by their enemies as amoralists, antinomians in fact recommended a religious attitude that is not inherently a moral one (e.g. faith), which they believed would *lead to* works of love – while direct pursuit of good works would lead only to self-righteousness. This description holds good of Martin Luther, as well as of more 'disreputable' antinomians such as the Ranters, of whom more later, or William Blake. Augustine's famous saying 'Love and do what you will!' can also be included, as indeed can the whole of Paul's Epistle to the Galatians, which influenced Luther so much. Luther's view is totally misunderstood if it is assumed that he was saying that we should choose to believe, and that this would be a meritorious act which would obviate the need for 'good works'. To put the record straight, it is worth looking more closely at his views.

Luther was no fideist: 'No one can give faith to himself, nor free himself from unbelief' (Dillenberger 1961: 25). He was not concerned with getting people to believe that God existed, since he could take it for granted that his hearers believed this. He was concerned with *confidence* – and that is what he, like the Bible, meant by 'faith'. He was quite explicit about this:

FAITH is not something dreamed, a human illusion, although this is what many people understand by the term. Whenever they see that it is not followed either by an improvement in morals or by good works, while much is still being said about faith, they fall into the error of declaring that faith is not enough, that we must do 'works' if we are to become upright and attain salvation. The reason is that, when they hear the gospel, they miss the point; in their hearts, and out of their own resources, they conjure up an idea which they call 'belief', which they treat as genuine faith. All the same, it is but a human fabrication, an idea without a corresponding experience in the depths of the heart. It is therefore ineffective and not followed by a better kind of life.

(Dillenberger 1961: 23)

Fideist faith is here rejected as just another work, and unfruitful in the production of further works. But real faith, he claims, is related to works, not as an alternative, but as cause to effect:

This kind of confidence in God's grace, this sort of knowledge of it, makes us joyful, high-spirited, and eager in our relations with God and with all mankind. That is what the Holy Spirit effects through faith. Hence the man of faith, without being driven, willingly and gladly seeks to do good to everyone, serve everyone, suffer all kinds of hardships, for the sake of the love and glory of the God who has shown him such grace. It is impossible, indeed, to separate works from faith, just as it is impossible to separate heat and light from fire.

(1961: 24)

But we do not do good works by trying to do them, as we should according to the moralistic paradigm. Luther's polemic against 'works' is a polemic against the moralistic paradigm – and an extremely insightful one. If you obey the moral law because it is the moral law, as the moralistic paradigm declares you must, you will hate it in your heart. Good works are only pleasing to God if they would have been done even if not commanded:

How can anyone use good works to prepare himself to be good when he never does a good work without a certain reluctance or unwillingness in his heart? How is it possible for God to take pleasure in works that spring from reluctant and hostile hearts?

To fulfil the law, we must meet its requirements gladly and lovingly; live virtuous and upright lives without constraint of the law, and as if neither the law nor its penalties existed.

(1961: 21)

The moralist is a person divided against themselves, secretly hostile to God and to goodness, and prone to all the vices of pharisaism. But 'the just shall live by faith', or as the modern translators have it 'one who is made righteous by faith shall live'.

I think Luther has undoubtedly got the New Testament on his side in this matter. He generally takes Paul as his text, but the gospels make much more sense on this reading too. No one who was not already committed to the moralistic paradigm could read the injunction to love one's fellows as a prescription for Kantian 'unshakeable goodwill'. It is an emotion which is being prescribed. The moralist will object: 'but emotions can't be commanded, since we can't *choose* to have them'; but only the moralistic paradigm tells us that a good life is something we can have by choosing. For the whole New Testament, it is most definitely not. Nothing could be more alien to the Bible or to the Protestantism of the Reformation than Kant's 'ought implies can'.

At this point I would like to take the discussion briefly to a more 'meta' level. While it is perfectly in order for the adherent of this or any other non-moralistic paradigm to refer to some actions as 'moral' and others as 'immoral', these terms have a different role from what they do in the moral-istic paradigm. For the moralist, there may be canons of proof that an action is the moral thing to do, and when this is shown, but not before, that action is prescribed, whatever other reasons there may be against it. But for non-moralistic ethics, no reasons for an action that did not already motivate that action, could motivate its description as 'moral'. The concept 'morality' becomes prescriptively redundant, epiphenomenal to any process of practical reasoning. But this in no way implies that morally good actions will be less likely from a adherent of a non-moralistic paradigm than from a moralist.

One last point about Luther: while his 'faith' is not cognitive belief, it is related to cognitive belief in that (1) it presupposes it; one can't have faith in what one doesn't believe in, or what one believes unworthy of confidence; and (2) if one has got the requisite beliefs, faith follows rationally from them, i.e. it is irrational, though possible, to hold the requisite beliefs about the being and acts of God and yet not to have faith. In this sense, Luther's religious paradigm of ethics is also a cognitive paradigm of ethics. The way to better morality is through truer beliefs. To this extent, Spinoza not Kant is the equivalent of Luther within naturalistic rationalism.

For Spinoza's cognitive paradigm of ethics is a non-moralistic one, the classic example of such within the mainstream of philosophy. He has shown that it is quite possible to write an *Ethics* from a non-moralistic standpoint – and how it is to be done: in the indicative.

Now it is necessary to look at the cognitive paradigm of morality in more detail, mainly with Spinoza in mind as the exemplar of this type of ethics, and to render it plausible. To this end I shall first expound the various theo-ries of moral psychology, defending (in my own words) that of Spinoza. The central contention of this moral psychology is that there is no such faculty as 'the will', and that the dualism of reason and emotions is a misplaced one. I shall then defend the plausibility of the resulting cognitive paradigm of morality, giving examples of various virtues and vices, and of moral struggle and conflict.

One classical model of moral psychology – the one that goes most natu-rally with the moralistic paradigm of morality – divides the soul into three faculties: reason, emotion (passion, inclination, etc.) and will. I take

Descartes as my example, but I fear a version of this theory was held by Augustine, of whom I shall have much to say in favour later.

For Descartes, reason may tell you what you ought to do, but the passions may be shoving you in the other direction – and reason lacks shoving-power. The will, though, has got shoving-power, and may carry out reason's behest (though, since it is free will, it may also decide to give way to the passions). As shoving-agent, the will has a task a bit like the spirited part of the soul in Plato. It is the policeman who forces the decisions of the legislator or judge (reason) on the unruly passions, since reason lacks the strong arm to do the job itself. However, as noted, the Cartesian will is also *free*. It is not an agent of reason, but an arbiter between reason and the passions. Nothing can *make* the will choose one way or the other. Indeed, one source of the popularity of the threefold splitting of the soul in this model, is that it guarantees 'free will'. But if this free will means that nothing explains the will's choice ('liberty of indifference') it seems more like randomness than like self-determination, which is arguably what we normally mean by freedom. We do not think a person unfree because they act in character, or in conformity with their opinions – quite the opposite. So a number of philosophers, including empiricists like Locke, Hume and Godwin, as well as Spinoza, have rejected the notion of the will as a faculty, and given another analysis of what is meant by 'will' and 'voluntary' in ordinary usage. 'It was done against my will' means that it was done contrary to my choice; it need not imply anything about the agencies of the soul that were working to make that choice. People's voluntary acts stem from their opinions, according to Godwin.

These theories reduce the faculties of the soul to two, reason and emotion (passion), but there are still several ways in which the two can be related. First, reason can be endowed with the shoving-power that Descartes denied it. Reason is seen as having its own goals, distinct from those of the passions, and these two powers shove each other till one wins. Until relatively recently, this view of moral psychology was always combined with the judgement that reason was the force of goodness, duty and altruism, while emotion (passion, instinct, inclination) was that of evil, immorality and egoism. Such, for instance, was Kant's view. Those who inverted the value-judgement and took sides with 'heart' against 'head' were seen as, and sometimes were, immoralists or amoralists. Today in popular judgement the reverse of Kant's view is often taken for granted. Not untypical, I think, was the view of a friend without any philosophical training who was telling me about the effects of his becoming a father: 'instinct takes over from reason' he said, meaning that the duties of care take over from egoism.

However we do not have to choose between these two judgements – between the heart and the head as the organ of virtue – since both rest on a false dualism. They both assume that reason and emotion are separate forces, each with their own aims and their own shoving-power. But has reason got independent aims or shoving power at all? Try as he might, the greatest modern spokesman for the view that it has, Kant, fails to produce any but formal imperatives out of reason, and fails to give any plausible account of rational motivation. The highest point he reaches – the notion of treating people as ends in themselves – can only be given sense when emotions have been introduced into the argument.

This brings us to the final false position in moral psychology: Hume's. Hume rightly recognises that reason gives no ends and no shoves of its own. But like the other philosophers that I have been considering, he treats reason and passion as separate faculties. If reason can't move us to action, it must be a 'slave of the passions': emotions dictate ends, reason only discovers the most effective means.

These theories can be summed up as follows:

1 *Descartes*

Reason   Aims, no shoving-power, good
Will   No aims, shoving-power, good or bad
Passions   Aims, shoving-power, bad

2 *Kant*

Reason   Aims, shoving-power, good
Passions   Aims, shoving-power, bad

3 *Popular romanticism*

Reason   Aims, shoving-power, bad
Passions   Aims, shoving-power, good

4 *Hume*

Reason   No aims, no shoving-power, neither good nor bad
Passions   Aims, shoving-power, either good or bad

It should be said that there is some simplification of historic viewpoints here for the sake of clear models: Kant seems to fit 2 in the *Groundwork* (Kant 1981), but actually comes closer to 1; no one thinks passions (or at any rate, inclinations) are always bad, only that they are bad if they conflict with reason. But most moral psychologies have approximated to one of these positions, or have slid between them.

Hume is right in assigning reason a purely cognitive task. But he is quite wrong about emotions. He sees them as being, at bottom, just blind urges, like itches which have to be scratched. But any real emotion or even desire, love or hate, fear or hope or anger or joy, lust or hunger or thirst – involves ideas, beliefs, judgements, explanations, all sorts of cognitive operations of reason. And these may be true or false, adequate or inadequate, well-founded or ill-founded. Of course they may not be – generally aren't – the results of conscious processes of reasoning, though they may be. I will come to the work of conscious reasoning in the next chapter. The point against Hume is that reason and emotion are not separate faculties, reason is implicit in all emotions. Only emotions can move us to action; but there are rational and irrational emotions. Here we have a fifth model:

5 Spinoza

Emotions   Aims, shoving-power, good if rational, bad if irrational

The faculties of the soul are reduced to one: emotion. Rather than reason being a separate faculty, rationality or irrationality are qualities of emotions. This moral psychology provides the twofold foundation for Spinoza's ethics: nothing can overcome an emotion except another emotion; but emotions can be more or less rational insofar as they are based on more or less adequate (cognitive) ideas – and it is sometimes possible to transform irrational into rational emotions by passing from inadequate to (more) adequate ideas. I think this position can be made clearer through a look at Macmurray's conception of reason and emotion, which forms the starting point of the next chapter. First, I want to show that the cognitive paradigm of morality is not so contrary to common moral experience as is often said.

In view of the short shrift usually given to the idea that virtue is knowledge (particularly today) it is surprising how many concepts that we simply could not do without in everyday moral discourse (particularly today) wear their cognitive character on their faces, while yet others can easily be shown to be cognitive, though their cognitive character may have been missed due to a narrow conception of knowledge or 'facts'. People and their actions and attitudes are described as considerate or inconsiderate, thoughtful or thoughtless, sensitive or insensitive, sincere or hypocritical, highly perceptive or downright ignorant. These virtues and vices relate in large measure to the interpersonal dimension of ethics. The self-regarding virtues will probably be more readily admitted to be cognitive in nature; and I have argued at length elsewhere (see my paper 'Scientific Socialism and the Question of Socialist Values', 1981, and my book *Socialist Reasoning*, 1990) that issues in the political sphere of practical reasoning are (logically speaking) cognitive ones, i.e. they are about which explanatory social hypotheses are true (which in no way contradicts the fact that people take sides in them largely out of class interest).

'Thoughtful', 'considerate', 'sensitive' (in the relevant sense) and (in many contexts) 'imaginative' form quite a close cluster of virtue-concepts. They all refer to knowledge of how another person feels. They imply, of course, that one also acts on that knowledge, and that such action is caring towards the other person. But we do not need to say 'thoughtful and kind' and so on. It is taken for granted that to be thoughtful is to be kind. A consistent non-cognitivist would have to object to this usage, and say that there was no virtue in being thoughtful, one needed kindness as well to motivate the actions usually called thoughtful. The usage seems to me quite appropriate. Thoughtfulness issues in kindness (other things being equal). Something similar occurs in the case of the other virtues listed here.

Another cluster of cognitive virtue-ascriptions, less directly other-regarding, are 'self-aware', 'sincere' and (for those touched by existentialism) 'authentic'. 'Self-deception', 'hypocrisy', 'inauthenticity' are likewise the names of vices. In all these, there is an ideal of transparency: that knowing, and disclosing by one's behaviour, what one is doing and why, is admirable. This is a cognitive ideal, and some might call it self-regarding: it is perhaps cognitively self-regarding, i.e. it is knowledge of oneself rather than of others that is at stake. But the applications of these concepts are usually in interpersonal situations. They do not (if anything does) come within the scope of 'things that affect only oneself' and so are 'nobody else's business'. Our ability to live a good life is largely dependent on the sincerity and self-awareness of others. I shall have much more to say about the existentialist idea of authentic existence later.

Some might claim that other-related vices come in two kinds: those involving insensitivity and those involving wilful cruelty. The callous person may lack cognitive skills, but what of the sadist? Surely, it is often argued, the sadist must be highly 'sensitive', acutely aware of his victim's pain in order to enjoy it. I doubt it. There is some evidence that many rapists are men who lack cognitive 'social skills': they cannot perceive the woman's refusal and horror as what they are, and describe their acts of violence as if they were acts of love. So far as Sade himself was concerned, he thought that sexual pleasure lay in causing another person to emit involuntary sounds – the sounds of orgasm or the sounds of pain. What then explains his preference for sounds of pain? Could it not be a fundamental coarseness of perception, like (to pass from the monstrous to the silly) that of someone who thinks that music is not music unless it is loud enough to permanently damage their ear drums.

It may be thought that this account trivialises evil, a question to which I must return. But to say that evil essentially involves cognitive error does not make it less evil – rather, it should make us take (certain kinds of) cognitive error much more seriously. Underlying the objection, though, is usually the fear that if evil is seen as stemming from defects of reason rather than acts of will, it will be seen as explicable, and as a result a certain kind of blame which can only be directed at the arbitrary conscious choice of evil will find no place. I am quite happy to accept this consequence; I follow the Four Great Jewish Heretics in holding that understanding is better than condemning; I refer of course to Jesus, Spinoza, Marx and Freud.

The opponents of the cognitive paradigm of morality often raise the spectre of the Cognitively Unflawed Villain, the person of unimpaired reason but evil will, as a counter-example. If the cognitive paradigm takes, not its Socratic form ('virtue is knowledge') but its Spinozist one (the transition from destructive to constructive emotions is best accomplished by the transition from false to true beliefs), then the mere existence of cognitively unflawed villains would not refute it, since such villains might not be reformable by non-cognitive means either. But the plausibility of the paradigm depends on villainy being at least typically dependent on cognitive flaws.

So can a realistic portrait be painted of a cognitively unflawed villain? I have suggested that the sadist is not a likely candidate, and this goes for psychopathic crime generally, whether 'crime' in the legal sense, or the great psychopathic political criminals. Hitler held beliefs about the Jews which were as far removed from truth and rationality as his feelings towards them were from human decency.

The most plausible candidate, I think, is the calculating capitalist who plunges whole communities into famine or war for the sake of a fast buck. But the structure of capitalist decision-making is such that this often happens without anyone deciding that it shall: the result is the cumulative effect of many profit-oriented decisions, unpredictable by the makers of any of those separate decisions. Even those clever and callous tycoons who really do have immense power are by no means cognitively unflawed. They may know enough about the effects of their actions to get their sums right and maximise their profits. But what do they know of the lives of their workers in a poor country halfway across the globe, who are forced into prostitution by low wages, or tortured in police cells for trying to organise a union? They may know that these things happen and not care, but it is one thing to know that such things occur, another to know what that means to the people concerned. I should perhaps add here that while an understanding of such a capitalist's defect as a cognitive one may make a certain kind of blame inappropriate, and alleviate the personal hatred we may feel for him, it certainly does not relieve us of the civic duty, if the opportunity arises, of executing justice upon him.

At this point, I may be accused of stretching the concept of the cognitive. The knowledge that Lord Moneybags lacks may be said to be 'empathy' or some kind of 'non-cognitive' understanding. But this is not so. Rather, it is that his knowledge is *sketchy*; the details that he lacks, which would bring home the real horror of his deeds, are as much facts as are the bare outlines that he knows about. It is of course very likely that he doesn't want to know, and also that he lacks imagination. The former is a question of epistemic ethics (which of course become the foundation of all ethics on my theory); and imagination, in the relevant sense, is a cognitive faculty, as Kant showed.

Nevertheless, it may be said, the sort of knowledge, and the sort of cognitive skill that I am talking about are of a very special kind: not for instance the sort of thing that can be learnt from books. I mention this since one sort of rejection of the cognitive paradigm of morality stems from a suspicion of book-learning − and along with this, though it is not the same thing, of causal as opposed to descriptive knowledge.

In fact, there is no sort of knowledge that can be learnt *entirely* from books, though there are sorts that can be learnt largely from them given a small experiential foundation, and others for which a larger experiential basis is required, books having a correspondingly more marginal place. Cognitive skills are learnt 'by living', as indeed is their lack. For defective cognitive skills are not always mere absences; they may be learnt inabilities to perceive things, 'resistances'. But it is not the case that these sorts of knowledge/unknowledge are impervious to reasoning and new information, and books can help. Oddly enough, academic non-cognitivists do often believe that cognitive skills and bits of moral knowledge can be learnt from books, if their use of examples is anything to go by; but only books of fiction. Yet if a great novel can sensitise a reader to features of human life that they had overlooked before, and can promote understanding of them-selves and others, so presumably can biography or documentary writing. But non-cognitivists usually stop short of admitting the capacity of explanatory, theoretical writing to improve us morally. Yet every novel has its explana-tions, implicit or explicit, and every decent work of psychology has its narratives. Freud noted the novel-like-ness of his own writing.

Behind the non-cognitive case that I am rebutting here, there are two false distinctions: between seeing different things and seeing things differ-ently, and between causal explanation and some kind of 'empathetic' conception of understanding or '*verstehen*'. To see things differently may be to see aspects of the situation that one had not seen before (or indeed to turn a blind eye to aspects of the situation that one *had* seen before), or to see that one had been mistaken about the facts, or that the causal relations between the various aspects of the situation are not what one had thought and so on. But to see the same aspects of the same set of facts in the same causal rela-tions as before, and yet to see them differently − what could that mean? Usually when this is said, the newly perceived fact is of a different sort from the others, and so is not seen as a new *fact*: it may be about how people felt, while the previous facts were all about their external circumstances; or about the hidden causes of the apparent events; or about the relations of the previ-ously known facts to wider aspects of the world. But these are all new facts, in the sense of objects of knowledge. I think that the idea of 'seeing some-thing differently' is often thought to be meaningful by analogy with perceptual gestalt switches. But the analogy breaks down, because gestalt switches only work by virtue of the conventions of representing three-dimensional entities two-dimensionally. This cannot be generalised to situations involving no such representation.

What about causal explanation versus *verstehen*? That understanding the causes of an event is not always *verstehen* can readily be granted. But perhaps *verstehen* does always analyse out into causal understanding? (I am taking it for granted here that intentional acts are typically caused by their intentions, and that intentions are typically caused by their agents' beliefs and desires).

I grant that there is a kind of brute *verstehen* which is not, or only marginally involves, causal understanding, namely recognising someone else's state of mind as one that one has experienced oneself. But this is not of crucial importance, epistemically or morally. It is important that our understanding of others be much broader than would be possible if we could only understand people of like emotions to ourselves. And indeed they are broader. The same man may be moved to tears by Shakespeare's Othello, and when he finds his own wife in bed with his best friend, may go and make them a cup of tea. The sympathy experienced in watching Othello is not bogus, nor is it some morally optional extra that helps us appreciate the arts but can be dispensed with in life. It is a distinct kind of understanding, independent of the ability to feel (in this example) jealousy, yet not limited to the knowledge that some people get upset if their beloved has sexual relations with someone else. If we could not extend our sympathies in this way, the moral prospects for humankind would be more hopeless than they are. For humankind is divided not only into two sexes, a number of sexual orientations, and a number of cultures, religions and ideologies, but also into as many (subtly or massively) differing emotional structures as there are people. If we can't learn to 'put ourselves in the other person's place' even though we could not conceivably be in that place, we might as well go a few steps further than the Nazis and separatist feminists, and all become hermits. This sort of 'putting yourself in the other person's place' involves explanatory knowledge; in the case of understanding distant cultures, I think this is obvious; but I also think that psychoanalytical explanations can help with the bridging of more personal gulfs in mutual understanding – for instance, in breaking down the intolerance to the traits of others that is borne of a reaction formation against the same traits in oneself. Knowledge – *episteme* – does not puff up, it builds up, though no doubt the Apostle was right about *gnosis*.

But it will be said: cognitive roads to virtue presuppose something non-cognitive. Yes they do. If we were not already 'conative' beings, and interdependent ones at that, no amount of knowledge could motivate anything. Having goals, having to co-operate, feeling sympathy – these are not virtues to be acquired, they are conditions of being human. They are not virtues in themselves at all: they are presuppositions of virtue, and exist even in the worst person. The worst person's sympathies may be limited, their co-operation exploitative, and so on. But sympathy, purposes, co-operation – these are givens. Their education, in a cognitive sense, builds virtues out of them.

Finally, the cognitive paradigm of morality may be thought to fail to do justice to the facts of moral struggle, in the sense of conscious effort to overcome the worst tendencies in oneself. And perhaps the somewhat 'sixties-ish' list of cognitive virtues in the last few pages may suggest by association that common heresy of the 1960s – that nothing which is attractive can really be evil.

It will be necessary to discuss this question again in connection with Augustine's doctrine that all being as being is good, and worthy of our love. Here I only want to rebut the suggestion that the cognitive paradigm of morality ignores the seriousness of moral struggle.

To be plausible, the cognitive paradigm must include an account of such struggle as *cognitive* struggle – a phrase which admittedly sounds a little odd. For if having explained freedom, not as the sheer act of will, but as the openness of our emotions and so also our actions to the effects of well-founded belief, we then backtrack and admit something like a 'will to believe', then all is lost. Whatever cognitive struggle might be, it can't be the struggle to make oneself believe something cognitively unfounded.

Let us take an example. A man has a persistent tendency to expect the worst. Naturally this makes him a lot less happy than he would otherwise have been. But it does not stop there. It weakens his resolve to make the world a better place, or even (more realistically) to help stop it getting worse as fast as it is doing. At his union meeting, he votes against a strike because he doesn't think it can succeed. He paid his poll tax because he didn't think the non-payment campaign would ever gain mass support. He doesn't give money to aid charities because he thinks it might end up in the pockets of corrupt bureaucrats. It affects his personal relationships too. If his wife is irritable, he thinks she is about to give him a full-scale row, and his conse-quent behaviour sometimes actually sets off a row which would not otherwise have happened. When a friend asks him an innocent question, he wonders how the friend might use the answer against him, and avoids replying.

It is clear that this tendency to expect the worst is a *vice*. It is also clear that it is *cognitive* in nature: to expect something is to believe (at some level) that it will probably happen. It may be pointed out to him that this is an unreasonable belief. Then begins the cognitive struggle against resistances to this new belief. Perhaps he comes to be completely convinced, at the conscious level, that his tendency to expect the worst is unrealistic. But the tendency does not go away forthwith. In each case the struggle to have reasonable rather than unreasonably pessimistic expectations has to be renewed. What C.S. Lewis (1955: 120–121) says about the 'virtue of faith' is relevant here: that it is not believing what you have no good grounds for, but believing what you know you have got good grounds for, even when it doesn't *seem* to be true. Take Shakespeare's Othello again: he had much better grounds for believing in Desdemona's fidelity than for disbelieving in it. But he 'let his suspicion get the better of him'.

At this point, someone may think that the cognitive paradigm of morality has broken down. Maybe expecting the worst is a cognitive vice, but if it can persist in the face of cognitive enlightenment, is not something else required, i.e. an act of will: the 'will to believe', not now as a substitute for good grounds for belief, but as a supplement to them?

My reply would be that it is indeed possible that a person's disposition to expect the worst might be impervious to cognitive enlightenment. But if so, there is no such thing as 'the will' to overcome it, for voluntary self-overcoming can always be analysed as the transformation of an emotion based on one belief into an emotion based on another. The disposition might still be overcome by some non-cognitive process – be it behaviour therapy, an improved sex life or a few pints of beer. But if it is to be overcome by the 'mind' at all, it can only be overcome by a change of beliefs *at some level*. As I have set the example up, a change of beliefs about whether the worst is actually the likeliest to happen has not been enough; but a change of world view (which I also take to consist of beliefs) or a psychoanalytical unearthing and working through of unconscious beliefs may do the trick.

And here we have come to two processes which it is surely quite natural to call 'cognitive struggle': the inner struggle between two conflicting world views – as recounted in Augustine's *Confessions* for instance – or psychoanalysis, in which everything works by becoming aware of what was previously unconscious, yet which is often a bitter struggle, and is not without its casualties, and fatalities too.

So much by way of removing some of the implausibility of the cognitive paradigm of ethics to modern 'common sense'. The next stage of my argument is to defend the Spinozan version of that paradigm by means of a critical analysis of Macmurray's metapsychology of morals.

3 Spinozism
The work of reason

My reasons for starting this part of the argument with a discussion of John Macmurray are best explained in terms of the various paradigms that I enumerated in the last chapter. To anticipate, I think Macmurray gives one of the best accounts of position 5, the Spinozist account, but nevertheless often slips into 3 (romanticism), perhaps because he is reacting so strongly against 2 (Stoic or Kantian rationalism). He is upgrading emotion by pointing out that reason is inherent in emotions, which can consequently have qualities which have often been attributed only to reason conceived as an independent faculty. But every now and then he attributes to emotion *as distinct from* reason, qualities that emotion can only have as inclusive of reason. This ambivalence about reason is characteristic of existentialism, to which tendency of thought Macmurray can be seen as belonging. He does not call himself an existentialist, of course – who does? – but he is closer to the other three major existentialist thinkers (Kierkegaard, Heidegger and Sartre) than to any other modern philosophers, and in many ways closer to each of them than they are to each other.[1] One aspect of his existentialism is this simultaneous rejection of the head/heart dualism and partisanship of the heart within it, and I shall shortly make an immanent critique of his thought with a view to refuting paradigm 3 and defending paradigm 5. But with this warning, I pass to Macmurray's excellent account of the place of reason in human emotional life. He defines reason as follows:

> reason is the capacity to behave in terms of the nature of the object, that is to say, to behave objectively.
>
> (1935: 19)

So defined, reason is involved in emotions, not just in 'thoughts':

> We are in the habit of saying that our feelings are just felt. They can't be either true or false; they just are what they are. Our thoughts, on the other hand, can be true or false. About that we have no difficulty. Yet, if we think carefully, we shall realize that there is no special difference between feelings and thoughts in this respect. ... True thoughts are

thoughts which refer properly to reality, and which are thought in terms of the nature of the object to which they refer. Why should our feelings be in any different case? It is true that they are felt and that they are what they are felt to be, just like our thoughts. But they also refer to things outside us. If I am angry I am angry at something or somebody, though I may not always be able to say precisely what it is.

(1935: 24–25)

Since emotions refer to the nature of the object, they can be true or false as much as thoughts can. But a word of caution is needed here: is it being said that emotions can be true or false because they include a cognitive element? That is the Spinozist position which I want to defend. Or is it that emotions are seen as having a relation to their objects which is analogous to the truth or falsehood of thoughts, but independent of it.

> In feeling emotions we feel the things to which the emotions refer. And therefore we can feel rightly or wrongly.
>
> (1935: 25)

Yes, in that the things may be or not be as the emotion takes them to be. In the example Macmurray has just used – fear of mice – the feeling is inappropriate because it is false that mice are dangerous. Fear of mice in some way involves the thought 'mice are dangerous', and therein lies its 'falsehood'. Of course, the person who is afraid of mice would not affirm that mice are dangerous, and for just that reason would be likely to recognise the irrationality of the fear. A psychoanalyst might say that mice are unconsciously believed to be dangerous, or more likely, unconsciously identified with something that is believed to be dangerous.

The practical importance of the question whether emotions are right or wrong *analogously with* beliefs or *because they involve* beliefs becomes clear when we ask how to put right irrational emotions. The Spinozist answer is 'by putting right the beliefs that they involve'. Now the person advocating an analogical relation between beliefs and emotions might reply 'but the person who is afraid of mice doubtless already holds the true belief that they are not dangerous, but acts as if they are'. The psychoanalytical account however allows us to deal with the problem in a cognitive way: by becoming aware of their unconscious identification of a mouse with a penis (or whatever), one comes to be able to order one's actions on the basis of well-founded beliefs. This is not a *purely* cognitive process: the emotions associated with the unconscious belief must be abreacted. But the becoming-conscious of the belief is what sets off the abreaction.

The first thing to note about Macmurray's characterisation of reason is that it preserves and accounts for the double character that the concept 'rational' has – like the concept 'moral': a descriptive and a normative character. We say 'humankind is a rational species', and we say 'Joe acted irrationally'. Joe could only act irrationally if he was a member of a rational species. The applicability of the descriptive notion of rationality is a condition of the attributability of either rationality or irrationality in the normative sense. But this does not mean that rationality and irrationality are two equally good ways of being rational in the descriptive sense, as being red and being green are two equally good ways of being coloured. Irrationality is a deficient mode of rationality (as Heidegger might have said, just as ignoring someone is a deficient mode of solicitude for them). How can we account for this two-sidedness of rationality, and the asymmetry of rationality and irrationality? Macmurray's definition does it very well. The descriptive notion of rationality – the rationality that distinguishes people from the beasts – is our behaving in terms of the nature of things 'outside' us; but our ideas of those things may be more or less adequate, according as we interact more or less sensitively with them. This is not an extra norm imposed on top of the descriptive sense of rationality. It is inherent in it. The drive to interact with 'other' beings more, and more sensitively, to act in terms of their nature, includes the project of *truth* in our ideas about them. Consider Macmurray's example:

> A little boy starts to run across a busy street. His mother sees him from the pavement and sees that he is in imminent danger of running in front of a motor car. Her natural impulse is to call out to him in terror. If she did so she would be acting subjectively in terms of her own natural constitution, responding to a stimulus from the environment. But she does not. She recognizes that to shout to the boy would only increase his danger by distracting his attention, so she suppresses her impulse. Her behaviour is rational, because it is determined not by her subjective impulse but by her recognition of the nature of the situation outside her. She acts in terms of the nature of the object.
>
> (1935: 20–21)

If the mother had acted 'subjectively', irrationally, she would still have been acting in terms of the nature of her child, the car, and the real threat posed by the car to her child: but in error about the nature of that threat. This feature of rationality as both fact and norm stems from the fact that *belief* is a psychological fact, and one which has its norm within itself: to believe is to hold for true, hence it fails if it is false.

Now I noted above that the twofold nature of rationality is shared by the concept of morality: a fox can't be immoral, because it is not a moral being. And rationality in Macmurray's sense is closely connected to morality.

> Morality, after all, is merely a demand for rational behaviour, and its difficulty is only the difficulty of overcoming our own natural bias in favour of ourselves and those we love, and demanding that life shall show us and them special consideration. Morality demands that we

should act 'in the light of eternity', that is, in terms of things as they really are and of people as they really are, and not in terms of our subjective inclinations and private sympathies.

(1935: 23)

Of course, all human action is in terms of how some other people or other beings are, in that it involves some beliefs about them, and, in the case of any action within the bounds of sanity, some true beliefs about them. But immoral action involves inadequate ideas about others. Action is moral insofar as it relates to others as they are in themselves, rather than as they are for us. But of course this is not any Kantian distinction between an unknowable 'thing in itself' and its appearances. The point is rather that what someone or something is 'for us' is a shot at an account of them as they are in themselves, and the shot may be nearer to or further from its mark. As what someone is for me is brought closer and closer to what they are in themselves, my actions towards them in the light of that knowledge will be more and more moral.

Now we must come back to the question of how this improvement of the understanding is brought about. Is this a cognitive process? Macmurray's answer hangs on his use of two pairs of concepts: knowledge and thought, and reason and intellect.

In *Interpreting the Universe*, Macmurray coins a philosophical slogan which sums up what might be called existentialist epistemology, though different existentialists would use different words.

All thought presupposes knowledge.

(1933: 15)

He comments:

This is a principle which is frequently overlooked in philosophical discussion. We construct theories of knowledge which imply that knowledge is the result of thinking, and that it is, therefore, essentially bound up with the processes of reflective activity. The simple observation that you must know something before you can think about it completely upsets the equilibrium of all such theories. It is because we know things and are interested in them that we think about them at all. And the reason why we think about them can not be in order to know them but at the most in order to know them better. The probable reason why the simplicity of this fact has often been overlooked is that our modern philosophy has been very largely concerned with the development of science. Scientific knowledge is, of course, the result of systematic activity of a reflective kind. In our consideration upon this we erect science into the type of all knowledge.

(1933: 15–16)

This point is clear and I think entirely correct. 'Knowledge' here means the knowledge that we all have as a result of our practical interaction with the world. 'Thought' means deliberate, reflective activity, 'working things out'; this is the source of all theoretical knowledge, including all science. The second distinction parallels the first, at the level of emotional and moral life: reason is inherent in the emotions as their reference to the nature of things outside us; intellect is the reflective work of practical reason. Macmurray is no empiricist about science: in it, theory precedes experience. But at the same time as it has misunderstood science, empiricism has also misunderstood ordinary experience by assimilating it to its own model of science: *just looking*, rather than practically engaged looking (looking for, looking out, looking after) has been taken as the paradigm. I don't know whether Macmurray had read Heidegger's *Sein und Zeit* but this is very like the account there: 'concern', our practical interaction with the world, has its own kind of looking, which Heidegger calls 'circumspection' (*Umsicht* = 'looking about'). Heidegger differs terminologically in that he reserves the word 'knowledge' for reflective knowledge and the 'just looking at' of empiricist perception-theory. 'Understanding' in Heidegger corresponds to pre-reflective 'knowledge' in Macmurray, while Heidegger's 'knowledge' is closer to Macmurray's 'thought'. But the point is the same: that the 'theoretical attitude' – reflection, contemplative perception, science – arises only after and on the basis of an extensive familiarity with the world derived from practical interaction with it. They also share an account of the origin of the theoretical attitude: both see it as arising from breakdowns or failures in our practical interaction with the world:

Life is essentially concrete activity. Thought involves the temporary suspension of concrete activity. It holds up the action of life. We *stop* and think. What is it, then, that brings about this stoppage of the normal processes of life-activity? What, in other words, is the general reason, or rather the general cause, of reflection?

The primary cause is some recognized failure in concrete activity. We stop to think because our undeliberate action has gone wrong, or because the immediate motives which normally determine the direction of action have failed. Suppose, for instance, that in walking from one village to another along a road with which we are unfamiliar we come to a fork in the road with no indication whether we should go to the left or to the right. We have been following the road which led to our destination. Suddenly it has become two roads and we are physically incapable of following them both at once. We are brought to a standstill. Our immediate experience provides no motive which will select one rather than the other. We are compelled to stop walking and to reflect.

(1933: 36–37)

The aim of thought is that the interrupted activity may be resumed (compare Heidegger's *Being and Time* sections 13 and 16).

These points of both Macmurray and Heidegger are quite correct, but they are the starting point for an error that both sometimes fall into. Although this error mainly concerns science, it is worth discussing since it has effects in their ethics too, for instance in Macmurray's account of intellect (as distinct from reason). The error is: that scientific knowledge adds nothing new to practical knowledge, which it merely spells out; but worse, in the course of spelling it out, it impoverishes it.

> We forget, in our preoccupation, that the kind of knowledge that science achieves is the result of investigating a world that we already know. The conclusions of some centuries of scientific research into the characteristics of matter constitute only a minute portion of our knowledge of the physical world. Men knew the world they lived in long before science was thought of. And in some ways, perhaps, they knew it better and more intimately than most of us know it today, since we took to living in towns and travelling in motor cars. That immediate knowledge of the world which is the effortless result of living in it and working with it and struggling against it has a much higher claim to be taken as the type of human knowledge than anything that science either has or can make possible. For the scientist takes this immediate knowledge of the world for granted and bases himself squarely upon it by his continuous appeal to facts. His particular business is simply to interpret it, to express it in such a way that we understand what we already know in a quite different and immediate fashion. The understanding of the world which we gain through science can never be a substitute for the experience of it that we have in the normal unreflective process of living.
>
> (1933: 16–17)

Most of this passage is also true enough; it is right to take practical knowledge as the starting point of epistemology; it is true that science abstracts from some facts in order to uncover others (e.g. to discover the causal mechanisms governing the world by *separating out*, experimentally or in thought, particular mechanisms from the others which co-determine the concrete course of events in the world with them). It is also true that without our initial practical knowledge of the world, scientific knowledge would have no significance for us.

But it is certainly not true that science adds nothing to our knowledge, but merely spells out what we already knew at the 'immediate' or prereflective level, which the phrase 'simply to interpret it' seems to suggest. Indeed, unless theoretical activity can correct and add to the practical knowledge that preceded it, how could it overcome the breakdown that gave rise to it, and allow practical activity to be resumed?

It may seem pedantic to pick Macmurray up on a few unguarded phrases like this, when he says plenty of things which indicate his regard for science as an irreplaceable source of much useful knowledge. But my reason is this: theoretical activity – science and reflective thought generally – is the *growing point* of our knowledge. This is the truth in the saying that we feel what our parents thought. As it stands, that saying implies a false contrast between thinking and feeling, but it is true, not only between generations but within one person's life, that changes in the twingey aspect of our emotions are slower than changes in the belief-aspect of our emotions. Someone who has come to believe that there are no ghosts may still get the shivers in a ruined abbey at midnight; someone who has relinquished an earlier belief in the wickedness of gambling may still feel anxiety when sitting down to play poker. Insofar as this is true, hostility to theoretical reflection – 'Don't think, feel' – is always conservative advice. It might be said: in an age like the 1990s when everything is getting worse, what's wrong with (lower case) conservatism? True enough, if one's beliefs are determined by contemporary fashions, it might be better to follow the emotions one learnt in younger days in a saner society. But if we take some trouble to acquire beliefs that are true, it is better that those beliefs are effective in their transformation of our emotions than that we should be suspicious of their effects as 'mere intellect'.

There are certainly passages where Macmurray is generous in his praise of science,[2] yet I think he sees its value (and that of 'intellect' generally) only as utilitarian, improving the means towards ends set by emotion, rather as Hume sees reason as a slave of the passions – but with the difference that for Macmurray, reason pervades the emotions too, so the dichotomy is not between reason and passion, but between emotions (which include reason) and intellect as a de-emotified mutation of reason, useful only in technical matters, including science. A clue to this is his hostility to 'knowledge for its own sake'. In a passage on education (in *Freedom in the Modern World*, 1932) he says such things as:

> All thought that is not *meant* to go beyond its conclusions to their application is unreal thought, and unreal thought is a monstrosity.
>
> (1932: 135)

> There is no significance whatever in knowing things just for the sake of knowing them and nothing more. The search for knowledge is either the search for that which has a vital significance for human life or it is a lapse into unreality.
>
> (1932: 135–136)

> Young minds should not be allowed to think in ways that are unreal for them about things that have no significance for them. But alas! our educational system has its own inertia and resists strongly. We still force

our young people to learn all sorts of things – we call it 'acquiring knowledge' – which have no significance for them and which never will have any.

(1932: 137)

It is easily possible to know too much. There are masses of things that we should refuse to know – and they are not merely the domestic affairs of our neighbours.

(1932: 137)

And again in an essay on education in *Reason and Emotion*:

Knowledge which is not learned in and through its application; knowledge which makes no immediate and recognized contact with action and life, is worse than useless.

(1935: 87)

How pernicious this would be as an educational policy depends on how loosely one interprets words like 'significance'. Children quite naturally take to stories about Robin Hood in Sherwood and King David in the cave of Adullam, about fairies and anthropomorphic animals, about space monsters and rogue robots, none of which have any direct relation to their lives. Of course one may say that they can relate to Robin Hood because they admire a friend who outwits the playground bully, or they like Pooh and Piglet because they have got soft toys and enjoy walks in the forest. But once we go down that road, there is no end to the things that they can connect in some way with their own experience, and the more diverse the things they can learn to connect with it, the better. If on the other hand one were to go down the opposite road – if one were to tell a class of white upper working-class children from Southampton only stories about white upper working-class children from Southampton, they would all be bored to tears, and worse, would grow up unimaginative and narrow in their sympathies. The drive towards 'relevance' in education is essentially a de-skilling device, a moderate version of the fantasiectomy practised in Zamyatin's novel *We* (1972). Just as *play* is both an end in itself and the chief way skills are acquired in young life, so cognitive play, whether imaginative fiction or knowledge of 'distant facts' such as the lifestyle of dinosaurs, the nature of the rain forests, black holes or the peasants' revolt, trains the intellect – that growing tip of practical knowledge and of the reason inherent in the emotions. It equips children to think beyond the dull routine for which they are being trained in their 'relevant' lessons.

To return for a moment to Macmurray's account of science: while it is closer to the truth than many of his contemporaries' accounts, and while he was of course in no way a specialist in the philosophy of science, it is useful to see where he goes wrong about science. Starting from the correct point that science is necessarily fragmented, he draws the following mistaken conclusions:

1   'the scientific attitude abstracts from emotion' (1935: 188). Of course, science tries to avoid its conclusions being deflected by wishful thinking under the influence of the emotions, and indeed Macmurray praises it for this: we should not be afraid of the truth. But sciences have no incapacity to study the emotions; and their results may evoke emotions in those to whom they are known.
2   That science can't study concrete individuals. This is odd from one who recognises psychoanalysis as a science, and whose own education included some training in geography. Science rather must pass through abstraction, but the end result is 'the concrete analysis of the concrete conjuncture' (Lenin), which is concrete because 'it is the union of the diverse' (Marx).
3   That 'science is not knowledge of reality' and 'is descriptive not explanatory' (1935: 187); and that it 'is always about how things behave, rather than about the things themselves' (1935: 190).
    Here Macmurray is I think accepting an empiricist or operationalist account of science. This is not the place to defend scientific realism, which I have said enough about elsewhere (Collier 1988, 1994) but the fragmentation of the sciences and their use of abstraction does not entail operationalism; the mechanisms discovered by abstraction (i.e. by abstracting from the operation of other mechanisms) may be features of reality, co-determining the course of the world along with those other mechanisms; these mechanisms are the structures of things, and explain how those things behave.
4   That scientific knowledge is impoverished in comparison with pre-scientific knowledge.

> In some queer way things depend for the knowledge of them upon our personal interest in them. So soon as we depersonalize our attitude to them, they withhold their secret and dissolve away into sets of general characteristics floating in an ether of abstract intellect.
>
> (1935: 152)

This is a half-truth. By itself, scientific knowledge would lack the significance of everyday knowledge, but it does not exist by itself, and can add to our concrete knowledge things that we could not have known without science. To know why a tree has got the shape that it has does not reduce but increases one's knowledge of the tree; to know that the sun is 92 million miles away does not stop it shining on us.

These non-realist points of Macmurray's about science are not meant as hostile to science but as putting it in its 'proper place'. But that place is a merely instrumental one. The ends towards which it is a means are set by the emotions. And this applies not just to science but to intellect generally. My emotions tell me to look after my son's health, my intellect finds out what foods are good for him.

This is another half truth. Science and the works of the intellect generally could not transform us or move us to action unless we were already emotional beings, whose emotions are not Humean twinges but Spinozan emotions which involve ideas referring to other beings – ideas which can be true or false, and can be contradicted by the findings of science and intellect generally. But since we are Spinozan beings, not either emotionless Daleks or Humean twinge-bundles, intellect can transform us and move us to action. And not just by showing us better means to existing ends: for it is the emotions themselves that are transformed by the transforming of beliefs intrinsic to them; it is not just the acts motivated that are changed by discovery of better ways of doing them.

Macmurray's playing down of the intellect in moral life is in the first place directed against Stoic and Kantian hostility to the emotions, and so far so good. But it leads him to talk about the education and liberation of the emotions as if this were parallel to, rather than an effect of, the achievements of free thought. Thus (admittedly in a popularising work – but much of his best work is popularising) he tells us that we are 'intellectually civilized and emotionally primitive' (1932: 43) which may be true enough in a sense, but only as another way of saying that we know a lot more about quarks and quasars than about our own unconscious or the feelings of our friends.[3] He goes on to say:

> Value is emotionally apprehended. We agreed, in setting thought free to discover truth, that we did not know what was true; but in keeping emotion bound, we refused to agree that we did not know what was good. By freeing thought we escaped from a false certainty and gained in exchange, not certainty, but the steady growth of real knowledge. By refusing to free emotion we have left ourselves in a false conviction about good and evil, about right and wrong, about what is worth while and what is not. In that all-important field we are still at the mercy of social prejudices, of traditional convictions. To set the emotions free, therefore, would mean that we began to doubt our convictions about what is good and what is not good.
>
> (1932: 46–47)

It looks here as if emotions are again being seen as *distinct from* beliefs, and their liberation as *parallel to* the liberation of thought by the Enlightenment. But how can the rectification of the emotions proceed other than by the rectification of the knowledge they involve? And if we start with suspicion of intellect, what are we left with to educate our emotions? Yet in the moral sphere, Macmurray has a suspicion of intellect akin to that of D.H. Lawrence (to whom he refers in this connection). For instance, in his article on 'The Virtue of Chastity' (in *Reason and Emotion*) he says:

> the orthodox European tradition of sex-morality, what we refer to as 'Christian' morality, is essentially external and intellectual. It is external *because* it is intellectual, for intellect is essentially external, objective, outward looking, dealing with external situations and the external world, and so *organizing* life in terms of external situations.
>
> (1935: 125)

But in what sense is intellect 'outward looking'? Macmurray has just been criticising the Stoics and Kant for their legalistic and anti-emotional morality, and goes on to say, in contrast to a Christianity which has become Kantism for the masses, that:

> what Jesus did was to substitute an inner and emotional basis of behaviour for an external and intellectual one. It was the externality of the Pharisee morality which he condemned. And his basis for morality was not rules, principles or laws, but love. And love is emotional, not intellectual. We are driven to the conclusion that our so-called 'Christian' morality is not Christian at all in the true sense, but Stoic, and that this is particularly true in our morality of sex.
>
> (1945: 125–126)

Now it is true that Jesus's contrasts between what Moses said and what he said, in the Sermon on the Mount, are contrasts between 'outer' and 'inner' in the sense that Moses commanded or forbade 'outward' actions and Jesus commands or forbids 'inner' emotions. But this is not a contrast between thinking and feeling; it is a contrast between doing and feeling. The sense in which the intellect is 'outward looking' is quite different; it is outward looking because it is the growing tip of reason, because it is trying to get it right about the nature of beings outside oneself, in accordance with Macmurray's own definition of reason and characterisation of morality quoted at the beginning of this chapter. Along with the Stoic and Kantian bathwater, Macmurray has thrown out the object-directed baby. If sexual morality means anything, surely it means being 'objective and outward looking' in making a serious effort to act in the light of how the other people involved feel.

To conclude this part of the argument:

- morality is about emotions;
- emotions are rational (in the descriptive sense) in that they include representations of other beings;
- they are rational in the normative sense to the extent that those representations correspond to how the other beings really are;

- the transition from irrational to rational emotions is the work of the intellect in discovering the truth about those beings with whom or with which we interact.

In saying 'intellect' rather than 'reason' I do not mean to play down the importance of non-reflective, non-discursive forms of reason in moral life. Perhaps the most valuable moral virtue one can possess is a quick, largely unarticulated but finely sensitive, skill in perceiving the emotions of another person. But I am talking here about *transitions* from irrational to rational emotions, and in these reflective intellect, as the growing tip of reason, is crucial.

These ideas are the core of Spinozism. Or at any rate, they are the core of paradigm 5 as defined in the last chapter, and it is to the elaboration and defence of that paradigm that this chapter is devoted. Allow me one more word here about my marriage of Spinoza to Macmurray. Paradigm 5 radically avoids head/heart dualism, but it is all too easy to slip back into that dualism, which has been so influential in European ethics. I have claimed that Macmurray, though his central thought belongs to paradigm 5, sometimes slips back into the dualism of paradigm 3 ('pro-heart' dualism). Spinoza also sometimes slips into dualism. When he does, it is into paradigm 2 ('pro-head' dualism). The marriage of Spinoza and Macmurray is meant to divorce Spinoza from the Stoic tradition and Macmurray from the romantic tradition; it is what the two have in common that I am defending.

As a preliminary to discussing Spinoza's ethics, I would like to show that Macmurray and Spinoza are also closer than might be thought in their epistemology. It might be thought that Spinoza's 'rationalism' is the extreme case of an epistemology in which thought precedes knowledge, and so diametrically opposed to Macmurray's. I think this is mistaken. I don't think he believed that knowledge could be derived a priori from axioms. That is his mode of presentation in the *Ethics* of course; but it is also his mode of presentation in his *Principles of Descartes' Philosophy* (both in Spinoza 1985), where many of the doctrines that he 'deduced' were ones that he believed to be false. Spinoza's epistemology follows from his ontology, not vice versa (and that is as it should be). According to his ontology, people are particularly complex entities, which can therefore interact in manifold and subtle ways with numerous other entities, and bear traces of that interaction; these traces, under the attribute of thought, are ideas of other entities. But initially, or as Heidegger might say *zunächst und zumeist*, 'in the first place and for the most part', they are ideas belonging to 'random experience', inadequate to their objects, or misassigned to an inappropriate object. Othello's jealousy does not reflect Desdemona's adultery but his own suspiciousness and credulousness. Reflective thought must get to work on them to transform them into well-founded ideas. Get to work *on them*: it pre-supposes them; 'thought pre-supposes knowledge' − but also, thought can correct pre-reflective knowledge.

If random experience (*experientia vaga*) corresponds to Macmurray's pre-reflective knowledge, we must here introduce an important notion of Spinoza's which I cannot find in any detail in Macmurray, though Heidegger has more to say about it. Random experience can be divided (analytically) into ideas derived from physical interaction with the aspects of the world that they are about, and ideas derived from hearsay. I would add that ideas in the second category prevail, both in constituting the greater proportion of knowledge, and in conditioning the way that physical interaction gives us ideas. As Freud has shown, even the unconscious speech of the body – in hysterical paralyses, for instance – is conditioned by language: what gets paralysed is a limb for which we have got a name – an arm or a leg – not a physiologically distinct system within the body. Empirical psychology has shown how perception is conditioned by language and by what the subject has happened to have learnt from hearsay. But its influence is deeper than that. When we fall in love, we fall in love in ways we have learnt from Shakespeare and the Song of Solomon and Bob Dylan, or at least from the anecdotes of friends and neighbours and family, or from the characters in our favourite TV soap opera. This does not necessarily debase our love – it may even ennoble it. It certainly doesn't make our love in any way false or 'second hand'. But it does mean that even so intimate a first-hand experience is preceded and conditioned by second-hand experience. This can be generalised: for every individual and in every respect, second-hand experience precedes and conditions first-hand experience.

The work of intellect, as the agency for fulfilling the norm implicit in reason, is to bring as much as possible of this mass of pre-reflective ideas into conformity with the truth about the beings of which they are ideas, thereby transforming the emotions in which those ideas inhere. Spinoza's rationalism is simply commitment to this work of the intellect, that: 'where id was, there ego shall be', as Freud put it (1971: 544).

I shall now discuss Spinozism in more depth, first (with reference to the attribute of thought) under the slogan 'moral education as explanatory critique of the emotions'. Then I shall ask what corresponds to rationality under the attribute of extension. The answer will bring us to the brink of the transition from the secular Spinoza (or the Freud of the object-libido/ego-libido theory) to 'the blessed Spinoza'[4] (or the Freud of the Eros/Thanatos theory).

An explanatory critique is an explanation of something which criticises it, not *in addition to*, but *by* explaining it. The central case is that in which a false idea of some aspect of a system is also an aspect of that system. For instance, Marx showed that the belief that wages are the price of labour is a false belief about an aspect of capitalism, and is also a tendentially necessary and functional aspect of capitalism; capitalism spontaneously generates this belief, and without its prevalence, capitalism would be destabilised. To show that the idea is false is (other things being equal) to criticise capitalism (as productive of and reliant upon falsehoods). Marx, Nietzsche and Freud all give explanatory accounts of various ideas such that to accept the explanation is either to reject the idea, or at least to reject the usual grounds for holding it to be true. It is this that has given them the name 'masters of suspicion', coined by Foucault or Ricoeur, I can't find out which.

But we should immediately make a distinction between two ways of using Marx's theory of ideology, Nietzsche's genealogy of morals and Freud's whole metapsychology and symptomology. For Marx and Freud (though perhaps not for Nietzsche) explanatory critiques are important because truth is important. Important no doubt in itself (they both had something of the disinterested scholar in them), but important also because 'the truth shall make you free': without a true conception of capitalism, the workers could not emancipate themselves; without a true understanding of our motives, we will remain prisoners of our neuroses. For Nietzsche, perhaps, truth was just a bludgeon to beat the moralists with and then throw away. But insofar as his arguments are convincing (a few of them are) it is because some of his readers still value truth.

Unfortunately, many people now take their cue from Nietzsche rather than Marx or Freud, and study ideas only with a view to 'explaining them away' as mere effects of some interest, with no concern for their truth. That sort of 'explanatory critique' is self-undermining, both because the critique only bites on the assumption that truth is aimed at, and because what a set of ideas is about is usually more interesting than the account of how the ideas came to be held.

The central case of explanatory critique as discussed by Roy Bhaskar is the case just outlined – the structure of falsehood – but he extends the account to many other cases in which to explain is to criticise (see his *Scientific Realism and Human Emancipation*, 1986: ch. 2, sections 5–8, and my discussion in *Critical Realism: An Introduction to Roy Bhaskar's Philosophy*, 1994: ch. 6. Bhaskar extends the notion further in various passages in his *Dialectic*, 1993). In Spinoza for the most part, and to some extent in Freud, we are dealing with a simpler phenomenon than that of structures of falsehood. It is helpful to introduce it as a theory of cause-object matching. In the case of Freud, this is not only helpful but true; in Spinoza's case an expository discussion is necessary to show that it is helpful rather than misleading; this I shall move on to afterwards.[5]

The theory of cause-object matching is best introduced with regard to several cognitive achievement-verbs, such as 'remember', 'see' and, in some senses, 'know'. An achievement-verb (I think the phrase is Ryle's) is a verb which indicates that the activity it refers to has succeeded; so that 'seek' is not an achievement-verb but 'find' is, 'argue' is not an achievement-verb but 'show' is, and so on. Take the case of 'remember' (not in the sense of remembering a fact, but of recalling an experience); there is clearly a phenomenological aspect to remembering which is the same whether the memory is real or not. But to say that I remember something is not just to report a current mental event, but to claim that the remembered event really happened, and that its happening caused the recollection. If someone proves to me that it never happened, I will retract the memory claim; I may still seem to remember it, but I will say 'I must have dreamt it', or something like that. This can be summed up by saying that the phenomenological phenomenon, the apparent memory, inherently involves a claim to be caused by its object; insofar as it presents itself as a memory, it presents itself as caused by the remembered event. In the case of knowing, we have a separate verb for the 'mental' side of it: believing. To believe is to claim to know, and to know is to believe something because it is true. Likewise in the case of seeing (and other perceiving too), to claim to see something is to claim that it is there, and caused the seeing. And the 'claim' aspect does not just arise in the verbal assertion that one remembers, knows, sees; it is inherent in the experience itself. All these cases involve a claimed cause-object matching; if the thing believed did not cause the belief, that belief is not knowledge; if the event seemingly remembered did not cause the 'remembering', it was not real remembering at all (and likewise in the other cases). The 'success' of the mental event is its matching of object and cause.

In the case of emotions, we do not redescribe them in the same way if cause and object do not match, but we do treat them as anomalous or irrational. The case is all too familiar in which someone is angry *with* their colleagues at work, but *because* they have had a domestic row, and so on. But we do recognise the irrationality of such displacement, and we sometimes suppress or apologise for our anger as a result. The reference here to *displacement* should alert us to the centrality of the issue of cause-object matching for psychoanalysis. According to Freud, the basic units of mental life are *wishes*, in a slightly technical sense: emotively charged ideas of some being (person or thing). A wish is an 'ideational representative' (*Vorstellungs repräsentanz*) which sounds daunting, but is a basically very simple concept. A wish is a representation (idea) of something and, because it is emotively charged, is also the representative in the mind of some instinct. For instance, sexual desire for someone is a representation of that person and a representative of libido. When repression occurs, the idea and the emotive charge are split apart and the idea excluded from consciousness. The emotive charge will be displaced on to some other object 'which is in some way or other suitable, much as our police, when they cannot catch the right murderer, arrest a wrong one instead' (1925: 314). The new object may be connected by a chain of random or irrelevant associations to the original, and in itself be very inappropriate. For instance, when I was 8 my schoolteacher was a snob and a bully who reduced a fair number of previously healthy children to bedwetting. Among her lesser sins was that she fancied herself as an elocutionist, and tried to get us to use 'spelling pronunciation', giving unstressed syllables the same phonetic value as stressed ones. Many years later, when TV newsreaders started talking in a similar way – calling soldiers 'sole deers' instead of 'sowjers' and Christians 'Chris tea-urns' instead of 'Chrishchuns', I found myself unreasonably enraged by it. After some reflection about this excessive reaction, I realised its real cause, and no longer feel anything more than mild annoyance at this affected diction.

As David Sachs has pointed out in his very valuable article 'On Freud's Doctrine of Emotions' (1982), Freud thinks that there is always an actual appropriateness between emotions and their causes/objects, no matter how inappropriate they may appear. Hence when the emotion is inappropriate to its apparent object we must assume that it is displaced from another object which is its cause. One description of psychoanalytic work is that it retraces the steps of displacement along its associative pathways until the emotive charge can be reunited with its cause as its object. It is then possible to deal with the emotion realistically, which it is not so long as the cause cannot be dealt with as object. In some cases, this may mean that a long repressed desire, now become conscious, can be satisfied; but in most, given the infantile nature of the repressed, it means that we can bring adult consciousness to bear on our memories of long passed problems, and free ourselves, to some degree, of their power. Once I had traced my anger to my teacher, I could reflect that that servant of Thanatos had long since gone to meet her master, and I had nothing to get upset about.

In itself, psychoanalysis is a backward-looking project of matching object to cause: undoing displacement. But its desired outcome is to free us from patterns of repression and displacement laid down in the past, and to free us for a forward-looking matching of objects and causes, i.e. enabling us to cause our aims to be realised.

I think anyone familiar with Spinoza will recognise something loosely Spinozist in my account of cause-object matching in Freud. Freud himself acknowledged his debt to Spinoza: 'My dependence on the teachings of Spinoza I do admit most willingly' ('Letter to Lothar Bickel', in Hessing 1977: 227). But there is a big problem about attributing the project of cause-object matching to Spinoza himself.

According to Spinoza, everything exists under two attributes (or rather two known to us), namely thought and extension. Under extension, everything is a material object, and under thought, the true idea of that object. But if idea and object are (transattributively) identical, how can the object be the cause of the idea (or vice versa)? I think I can answer this in three stages.

Stage 1: although Spinoza's theory of the transattributive identity of idea and its object is logically incompatible with interactionism (i.e. with the idea that mind and matter have effects on each other) it is for practical purposes equivalent to interactionism. As I put it elsewhere:

> While of course there can be no *causal interaction* between ideas and bodies for Spinoza (since they are transattributively identical), the practical consequences of his theory are very like interactionism. For if event E^1 at time T^1 causes event E^2 at time T^2, then since both events must occur under both attributes, everything is as if (for example) E^1 under

the attribute of thought caused E^2 under the attribute of extension. Effectively, an idea can, via my having of it, cause my actions and their physical consequences.

(Collier 1991b: 90)

This argument works both ways, i.e. for physical causes of mental events too.

Stage 2: nevertheless it may be said that, even if mental and physical phenomena – ideas and material objects – may (for all practical purposes) be said to cause each other, this causal relation cannot hold between an idea and *its* object. This sounds plausible, but I am not so sure. Suppose A (which of course exists under both attributes, as the idea $A^{thought}$ and as the body $A^{extension}$) causes B ($B^{thought}$ and $B^{extension}$); and suppose it is by virtue of (for example) physical properties that this causing occurs. Would it not be true to say that $B^{extension}$ caused $B^{thought}$? Spinoza would not say this, but it seems a natural enough usage given his two-attribute theory. Rather as, if Brutus in killing Caesar-the-ambitious-dictator also killed Caesar-his-friend-and-benefactor, one might say that his killing the ambitious dictator was the cause of his killing his friend. Certainly, Brutus did not stab Caesar because he was his friend but because he was ambitious; it was because he was ambitious that Brutus' friend died. If we are inhibited about saying also that the killing of the ambitious dictator caused the killing of the friend, I think that may be nothing but the voice of a Humean superego which it is high time we stifled. To give a more theoretical example: the father of Russian Marxism, Plekhanov, who described Marxism as a species of Spinozism, has a similar account of historical materialism. He rejected the division of the social whole into 'factors' (economic, political, ideological and so on), saying that all these things were inseparable aspects of the same developing social whole; but the laws governing its development were economic, not political or ideological. While this is not my reading of historical materialism, it is I think a coherent and not implausible one; and it is quite natural to say that it treats the economic as the cause of the ideological and political, even though the three are perhaps conceived as 'transattributively identical'.

Stage 3: the identity of an idea and its object seems on the face of it to present difficulties about error. If Spinoza's theory of truth is an identity theory – an idea is transattributively identical with its object – how can an idea be false of its object? Spinoza certainly thinks that many of our ideas about objects are inadequate; but he does think that they are all in some way true *of their objects*. The problem is that we misassign them, rather as we may have an accurate map but orient it incorrectly. Thus if I think I can hear the fire bell ringing because I am suffering from tinnitus, I am misassigning an idea which is true of my eardrums (or whatever) to the wrong object, the fire bell. Here the difference from my earlier account of 'wrong objects' may be only terminological: Spinoza says the eardrums are the object, the fire bell only the apparent object; my earlier account says the fire bell is the object, the eardrums the cause. Spinoza's usage ties in with his tendency to define things causally: we know what a circle is when we know the geometric prescription for drawing one. Just as Freud thought that an emotion is always appropriate to its causing object though not necessarily to its immediate, conscious object, so Spinoza thinks that an idea is always adequate to its causing object though not necessarily to its apparent object. If – and only if – we explain our ideas correctly, we will define them correctly, assigning them to their causes which will then be recognised as their true objects.

For Spinoza as for Freud, then, the move from irrational to rational involves becoming aware of the real causes of our ideas, so that causes and objects become aligned, and our emotions appropriate to their objects. In one sense, this involves a move towards more self-determination of the individual who becomes more rational. Their ideas are no longer put there by accidental events beyond their control, but become more and more susceptible to conscious testing by thought and action. In another sense, it means that our ideas of other beings are no longer determined by subjective distorting forces, but by the real nature of the other beings. 'That there may be ego where there had been id' is also that there may be reality-testing where there had been projection, and that there may be object-libido where there had been ego-libido (narcissism). This will become clearer if we view this whole process of becoming more rational, which I have so far set up in purely mentalistic terms, under the attribute of extension.

I take it that for Spinoza, the fact that we are rational beings is the same fact (under the attribute of thought) as the fact (under the attribute of extension) that we are able to affect and be affected by much of the world in many ways. So to become *more* rational – to have more adequate ideas and more rational emotions – is to interact more effectively and sensitively and over a wider range.

Our ability to interact so well is due to our physical complexity. For Spinoza, we are neither simple indestructible Cartesian consciousnesses, nor Humean reflectors lacking self-constancy. We are complex unities, composed of many less complex entities. What unites the parts of an individual and makes them an individual is a relatively constant and self-replicating pattern of interaction between its parts.

But relatively stable systems of interacting parts are not the sort of being which can have clearly defined boundaries. Not only an organism, but an organism's environment considered as an eco-system, may be such a system. Insofar as we depend on and interact with our environments, our environments are our bodies. I have defended this view at greater length in my articles 'The Inorganic Body and the Ambiguity of Freedom' (1991a, where I link it with Marx's dictum that nature is our inorganic body and with Heidegger's conception of *Dasein* as Being-in-the-world), and 'The Materiality of Morals' (1991b). The self, on this view, is a relatively centred but open-ended structure, 'a cross, not a circle'.

This conception is inferred from Spinoza's premisses; I do not claim that he consciously drew this conclusion from them. But it does make sense of what would otherwise be his biggest paradox: that our minds are composed of our ideas *and our bodies of the objects of those ideas* (or put the other way round, that the mind is the idea of the body). If 'body' is taken in this extended sense, then those things with which I interact enough to have adequate ideas of are parts of this body. I have argued that the extended body so conceived is (1) of indefinite boundaries: a matter of more or less part of one, not altogether or not at all part of one; (2) not an exclusive possession, since it overlaps with the bodies of others; (3) capable of expansion and contraction.

It is this last point that I want to take up now. If I become more rational, I interact with more things. They thereby become more part of me; my body is extended parallel with the extension of my mind by the latter's acquisition of more, and more adequate, ideas. And such a parallelism is just what a good Spinozist ought to expect.

Now if more of the world becomes more part of my body, how does that affect my *conatus*, my drive to persist in my being (and to expand my power to persist in my being)? First, it must be said that, in the light of what has been said here, a human conatus must itself be conceived (under the attribute of extension) as a drive for greater interaction, that is, both interaction with more things and hence greater extension of the part of the world that counts as part of the extended body, and greater interaction between the parts of that body; in short, greater extent and integratedness of the (extended) body. Under the attribute of thought of course, the conatus is a drive for clearer understanding, for rationality.

But insofar as the conatus realises its tendency, it becomes the conatus of an extended entity. It comes to include the drive to preserve the being of its new parts also. It becomes care for one's environment – care of the same sort (though not necessarily to the same degree) as our care for our own bodies in the narrow sense. And this is plausible enough in many homely instances. The more one is involved with something (say, one's garden) through sensitivity of perception and active work, the more one will care about the fate of its contents.

Plausible or not, someone may reasonably say: why should we accept these conclusions which (even if we accept your arguments) follow only from Spinoza's premises, many of which do not commend themselves to everyone? By way of a partial reply, I would like to say that, while in some parts of this chapter I have used a number of Spinozan concepts, not all of them are required to support the conclusion. What I am propounding can be set out as follows:

1   The general model of reason proposed by Macmurray: the capacity to behave in terms of the nature of the object;
2   An account of the 'inner' or 'mental' side of the norm of rationality as cause-object matching.

The link between 1 and 2 is a certain theory of error; when we do not act in accordance with the nature of objects, it is because we misassign our ideas to objects which are not their causes, and act towards the (non-causing) object in ways appropriate to the cause rather than to it.

3   An account of the 'outer' or 'physical' side of the norm of rationality as greater – more effective, sensitive and extensive – interaction with the world.

The link between 2 and 3 is the assumption that having true ideas cannot be an accident, but must be the result of better interaction with that of which they are ideas, than the interaction which would leave us with false ideas about those things.

4   An account of the unity of a human individual as a composite unity constituted by the relatively stable causal interaction of their parts. On the basis of these points, I have arrived at
5   The extensibility of human individuals as they become more rational/interactive, to include more of the world in the open structure that makes them the individual that they are.
6   The consequent tendency, as one becomes more rational/interactive, to care more for more of the universe, as it becomes more integral to one's own being.

This brings me to the final point of this chapter. The conatus or tendency to persevere in our being, which for humans takes the form of a tendency towards rationality/interaction, is of course finite, but it has no fixed limit in itself; the only fixed limit to its extent is the whole of being, although of course this is astronomically beyond our actual interactive worlds. It is possible however to extrapolate a regulative idea inherent in this conatus, the idea of what that conatus would become if it (impossibly) reached its limit. It would become a drive towards the persistence in being and integration of the whole universe. This is our first brush with the black cat referred to in the preface: Freud's Eros, Empedocles' Love, Spinoza's pantheistic Providence which is manifest only in the conatus of all creatures, or the love of God as Creator in Augustine's theology. Four quite different things ontologically, but equivalent as regulative ideas for human conatus. In the words of MacDiarmid's poem (which I trust will not be thought sexist, since the idea is reversible):

A'thing wi' which a man
Can intromit's a wumman,
And can, and s'ud become
As intimate and human.

And Jean's nae mair my wife
Than whisky is at times,
Or munelicht or a thistle
Or kittle thochts or rhymes.

He's no' a man ava',
And lacks a proper pride,
Gin less that a' the warld
Can ser' him for a bride!

(1967)

Perhaps this is the place to answer two related objections which have occurred to a reader of an earlier manuscript of this book, both of which stem from a different metaphysical position from the one defended here.

1   The logical objection that if one entity incorporates another, they cease to be two separate entities; but for entities to interact, they must be separate. Yet I write as if to interact with something is to incorporate it.
2   The moral objection that our incorporation of nature is exactly what an ecological philosopher ought to object to. The point is rather to let things be. This is essentially the same objection that has been raised by a number of ecological philosophers against Marx's idea of nature as our inorganic body: is this not just another form of anthropocentrism? (The two ecophilosophers who I feel closest to, John O'Neill and Ted Benton, both raise this concern). Surely, it is argued, it is just the independence of things outside our bodies which is the foundation of the respect we owe them. We may do what we will to our own bodies to an extent that we may not to anything else.

I think both these objections rest on the assumption that there is only one level of real entities in the world. I am assuming on the other hand that not only is, say, a biological organism a real entity, but so are the organs of which it is composed, the cells of which they are composed, the molecules ... and so on. Also, the societies into which certain organisms are organised (whether humans or bees in their hive or coral polyps) are real, concrete entities. Higher-order concrete entities (or to use Spinoza's term, 'composite individuals')are constituted as such precisely by the *interaction* of the lower-order ones. When a human being, considered as a 'body-actual', that is the body within the limits of the skin, interacts with other beings, it thereby incorporates them into its being (considered as a 'body-cosmic', the body which includes the world insofar as it is *its* world). What we call 'mind', in the psychological rather than the Spinozist sense of the word, is just this feature of the body-actual, that it interacts with other entities and thus incorporates them into its body-cosmic. That body-cosmic is also a concrete entity, a composite individual, though a higher-order one than the body-actual. The idea of incorporating, by interacting with, the whole of nature is of course only a regulative idea, the unapproachable limit of this process.

It is consistent with this notion of interaction/incorporation that one may incorporate something to a greater or lesser degree. It is not an all or nothing thing, like eating an apple. The clothes that I am wearing are much more part of me than the raspberry canes on my allotment.

Also, the causal 'interaction' between two entities may to all intents and purposes be one-way. If I gaze at a distant star in the night sky, it in some degree becomes part of me – what I am comes to be in some small measure constituted by it – without the star itself being affected at all. I do not incorporate it as I do the apple. Indeed, it may have ceased to exist millions of years before I was born, or may continue to exist for millions of years after I die. So, far from being an anthropocentric view of the so-called external world, this is an exocentric view of humankind.

APPENDIX TO CHAPTER 3: AGAINST IRRATIONALISM

I have described rationality as a norm inherent in human emotions, and I have touched on one motive for irrationalism, namely acceptance of head/heart dualism, combined with rejection – indeed inversion – of the pro-head value judgement that usually went with such dualism in past times. I shall return to this form of irrationalism (the 'paradigm 3' of last chapter) to discuss its infiltration of psychoanalysis later in this appendix. First I want to look at four other forms of and motives for hostility to reason. The first is closest to *lumpen*-irrationalism – the fear of having one's prejudices or wishful thinking overturned. The second and third are like paradigm 3 in that they rest on a false dichotomy. The fourth presents some real moral problems to which I don't know all the answers, but I don't think it gives any grounds for impugning reason as defined here.

Irrationalism as epistemic amoralism

'Epistemic ethics' is concerned with what one ought to believe, and while the detailed answer to that question is extremely complex, the ground of any rational answer must be 'one ought to believe what is true'. In one way, this maxim is an 'other things being equal' maxim, like all practical maxims. I do not agree with Kant that it is always wrong to tell a lie, though I am sure it is much more often wrong than is usually supposed in our utilitarian culture. And it is sometimes right to leave someone in 'blissful ignorance' when enlightenment would be unbearably painful for them.

But in another way, 'one ought to believe what is true' is an absolute. For one cannot sincerely say: 'I believe it, but it's not true.' Any account of beliefs which ignores the fact that they are truth-claims, fails to talk about beliefs at all, for to believe is to hold that the world is in such and such a way, and would be so whether one believed so or not. To treat of beliefs without reference to their truth or falsehood, as relativistic forms of the sociology of knowledge do, is simply to offer a gratuitous insult to people's opinions.

By 'epistemic amoralism', I mean the view that we should ignore the question of truth in forming our beliefs. The objection to it is essentially that it has to be a form of self-deception. What are we to make, for instance, of someone like Tertullian who says: 'I believe because it is absurd'? What is absurd presumably can't be true or, on a milder reading of 'absurd', can't have good grounds for being believed. Of course, Tertullian is not committing a formal contradiction, since 'Tertullian falsely believes that P' contains no contradiction. But said by Tertullian, it is surely a *lie*. One can easily imagine circumstances under which it would be a straightforward lie: if Tertullian said to someone who did not know who he was 'Tertullian believes that because it is absurd'. Tertullian would in that case be giving the other person to believe that the belief in question was false. If he really believed it true, that would be a lie; if he believed it to be false, he would still be lying – this time about his own belief. But since in fact he openly said '*I* believe because it is absurd', one can only describe him as lying to himself out loud. The *motive* for such self-deception remains a problem; perhaps it is a Pascalian wager with this difference: that the odds against are seen as much higher – but the stakes so high as to make this still a worthwhile bet, to escape even the slenderest chance of hell. There is certainly nothing admirable about such cowardice.

But it would be misleading to suggest that such epistemic amoralism is normally associated with religion, though some recent philosophers of religion have defended a form of 'fideism' or the 'will to believe' i.e. the justification of belief partly on non-cognitive grounds. It is usually secular, and indeed as carefree and egoistic as any other form of amoralism. Philosophers like Feyerabend and Rorty seem to value 'freedom' to 'believe what we like'; to choose, as the fancy takes us, whether to believe the findings of rational inquiry, or whether to believe that toadstools are put there by fairies, that the Tories care about the sick and homeless, and that the earth is filled with orange marmalade. All the objections to 'authority' – i.e. to the right of the powers that be to dictate our states of mind – that historically were the consequences of rationalism, get turned against reason and science as if these were just new forms of intellectual tyranny. But if I cannot believe the three absurdities mentioned in the last sentence but one, it is not because anyone or anything is constraining me, but because to entertain these propositions in the face of the overwhelming evidence against them would not be to believe them, but to *pretend* that they were so. The 'reason' that prevents me from believing them is not some external cognitive authority; it is rooted in the nature of belief – ultimately in the nature of the way we are in the world.

The illusory sort of freedom that Feyerabend and Rorty want to secure for us is the same as the 'cognitive freedom' posited by that degenerate form of the philosophy of religion 'fideism', according to which God deliberately tampered with the evidence for his existence in order to keep us guessing – as if I would increase your freedom by telling you: 'I might accept your invitation to dinner or I might not – I won't tell you before the night so that you can be free to believe what you like.' Such cognitive 'freedom' is clearly a loss of real freedom; it is itself a constraint.

Fideism (when explicitly so called) is usually concerned with 'choosing' one's religion, but that cannot be a correct description of religious convincement. If I could choose my religion I would worship trees, but this is no more a real option than believing that the earth is filled with marmalade. Neither can I choose my moral beliefs, even on issues about which people in my culture differ. For instance, knowing what I do about homosexual relationships, I could not possibly choose to regard them as immoral.

The real function of 'fideism', of the idea that belief can be a matter of will, whether in religion, morality, science or any other area of opinion, is to protect first-order dogmatism by means of second-order scepticism: a person's existing views, though they may be unthought-out prejudices, need not be subjected to critical reflection if one dogma is cognitively as good as another and the issue between them is a matter for arbitrary choice.

Likewise, non-realism in the human sciences often preens itself on its anti-dogmatism, in that it does not make truth-claims. But when a human science does make truth- claims, it thereby lays itself open to criticism – if contradictions can be found in it, or the weight of evidence is against it, it must answer its critics or make way for better theories. A theory which makes no truth-claims, on the other hand, is serenely immune to criticism – a dogma in the worst sense. And the claim that no truth-claims are being made is part of the meta-discourse of the theory; at the first-order level, its propositions can be given no sense at all unless they are read as telling us what is the case. This answers the question how, if my arguments are sound, epistemic amoralism can have any effects at all, since no one really believes it. It has the effect of protecting, at the meta-theoretical level, first-order theories which nevertheless carry on as if they were about objective truth; it declares any claims that they are false out of court and insulates them against revision or refutation.

Reason and authority

Both adherents of paradigm 3 and epistemic amoralists cast reason in the role of authority, and themselves in the role of liberators from or rebels against authority. So it is salutary to remember that for the age of reason and the Enlightenment it was precisely with authority that reason was contrasted – and they had, historically as well as philosophically, much more claim to be considered liberators than the romantic rebels against reason ever did.

However the reason/authority opposition is a false one, just as the reason/emotion opposition is. Just as we should not counterpose reason to the emotions but rational emotions to irrational emotions, so we should not counterpose reason to authority but rational to irrational authority. This ought to be obvious today when the larger part of epistemic ethics is about determining which authorities to believe about issues which one could never judge in any other way. Yet the mistake of the rationalists and enlighteners was historically very understandable. The late medieval philosophers had divided knowledge into natural or philosophical knowledge, which could be known by reason, and revealed knowledge, which had to be accepted on the authority of the Church. The enlighteners were right that the scope of reason should not be so limited; all received 'knowledge', whether learnt from Aristotle or the Church Fathers, should be subjected to the criticisms and tests of reason and practice. But this reflective, critical use of reason presupposes that we already have a body of knowledge, largely received from authorities (reliable or otherwise) to work on. The liberation of reason *should* have taken the form of saying: there is no knowledge without opinions received on authority, but all such opinions should be subjected to the criticisms of unfettered reason, to sort out the reliable from the unreliable authorities, rational authority from irrational. By attempting instead to start from scratch, the rationalists and empiricists simply hid from themselves the sources of their own knowledge, and presented a truncated fragment of received opinions as rationally or empirically demonstrable certainties.

Irrationalism as 'action not words'

The slogan 'action not words' is sometimes used to block criticisms of some course of action, and functions as an irrationalist slogan, often in conjunction with 'pro-heart' dualism or partisanship of authority against reason, (heart or authority being associated with action). The image that the appeal for action not words is meant to invoke is (negatively) the ridiculous spectacle of people engaging in endless talk instead of taking the action that they are talking about (obviously a pathological phenomenon, and correspondingly rather rare), or alternatively the professing of some ideal which the professor does nothing to adhere to in practice; and positively, of brave and honourable action for noble ends. But the situations in which it is invoked are rarely like that. Insofar as they are, the slogan is not irrationalist, since it is rational to act on one's beliefs. Indeed, the slogan is often guiltily implicated in its own negative images: one of the more common nuisances in 1970s radical circles was the person who spent all their time going to conferences and day-schools, talking endlessly about the fact that we ought not to be at conferences and day-schools talking endlessly, but out on the streets doing (unspecified) things. The irrationalist point usually implicit in the slogan is that talking – or thinking – about something somehow incapacitates one from doing it: that 'the native hue of resolution/

Is sicklied o'er with the pale cast of thought' (*Hamlet*, III.i). The switch from
the reasonable reminder that the aim of (certain kinds of) thought is to lead
to action to the irrationalist denial of the value of thought to action is sometimes made through some form of the menu/meal contrast: you can't eat a
menu; true, but you are not usually given a menu *instead of* a meal. 'Some
things cannot be said, only done' said the Oakshottian D.J. Manning (1976:
87); if this means that talking about storming the Winter Palace will never
lead to soviet power by itself, it is true and rather obvious; if it means that
the Winter Palace could have got stormed without anyone talking about it,
it is nonsense. And Manning seems to mean the latter: he even says that
Lenin's Marxism could not have influenced his revolutionary career, since
one is theory and the other practice (1976: 88).

As against this it needs to be recognised that the relation of theory to
practice is that theory can transform practice; it is the growing point of
developing practice, and the means of correcting faulty practice. The situation is parallel with the cases of reason/emotion and reason/authority: the
contrast should not be between reasoning and action, but between rational
and irrational action. The function of denouncing reason in the name of
action is to defend an irrational or outmoded course of action from criticism
and transformation.

The most natural place for action-irrationalism is in the self-defence of a
military commander who has been subjected to criticism in parliament for
his war crimes, or of a trade union official whose high-handed way of
running things is under discussion by the members. They say 'I am the man
of action, you are just talkers', and go on doing things the same old way.

Universal and particular

Reason is often associated with universality against particularity; although
there is nothing in Macmurray's definition of reason, which I have adopted,
to support this, he does assign reason such a function in the passage on
morality (1935: 23, quoted above, and 49–50). And on the one hand, there
are many contexts where such a function of reason is very welcome.

Reason as defined by Macmurray can be connected with universality in
this way: to know the real nature of objects, we need to explain them. We
ask questions about why they are as they are and do what they do. But
explanations are universal in the sense that they account for particular things
in general terms: if B behaves differently from A, it must have some features
that explain this difference; if A had that feature, it would behave that way
too. In the moral context, this leads us to question the different treatment of
different individuals; if A is treated differently from B, what feature of A
justifies that difference? If none is found, the different treatment is declared
unjust. Rationalism, historically, tends to be against racism, sexism and
nationalism. And this has been the main source of hostility to it on the part
of political reactionaries. Hostility to this aspect of reason is still deeply

destructive. When I read articles by self-styled left-wingers who argue for a 'militant politics around different identities' I am inclined to mutter 'send them to Bosnia or Rwanda'. The quest for the unity of humankind is the noblest legacy of Enlightenment rationalism (though it did not originate there – it is implicit in Amos and in the Cynics). And it is a lesson which very much needs to be re-learnt in today's politics. Even the idea that each oppressed group ought to be fighting for itself rather than for the emancipation of all the oppressed, seems to me regrettable. It is wonderfully satirised as 'dwarfs for dwarfs' in C.S. Lewis's Narnia story *The Last Battle*. If we ever get the Left off the ground as a serious political force again, let it be academics who fight for the railways and railway workers who fight for the universities, men who specialise in feminism, and whites who make it their priority to fight racism.

On the other hand, we are finite creatures, 'thrown', as Heidegger says, into some particular time and place and community, with particular friends and families, and so on. To follow Godwin's idea that the word 'my' should have no place in ethics – that I am no more beholden to my friend or my child or my lover than to any other person – would be inhuman. We cannot love humankind, we can only love a few people, and if we don't put them first, we will love no one. And something similar may apply to regional, national or ethnic traditions; if we try to situate ourselves, or our children, in them all, we lose them all.

We need to ask what makes universalism desirable in one context and particularism in another. It must I think be conceded to particularism that the sort of patriotism like Chesterton's, which loves England simply because it is *my* country, is a good deal healthier than the sort, like Kipling's, that loves England because it is 'the best' country. (I am assuming that patriotism on this island means loving England or Scotland or Wales, not loving the United Kingdom, which no one but a politician could profess to do except in jest). The latter is bound to lead to imperialism and other crimes against international justice; the former can just as well motivate shame at the iniquities of my country. I think we can go some way towards saying how we should be universalists and how particularists, if we recognise (1) that the suitable occasions for particularism have to do with love, while the occasions for universalism have to do with justice; (2) that the rationale of particularism is that we can love only particulars, and only a limited number of particulars. But the expansion of our boundaries described at the end of chapter 3 means an expansion of the number of particulars that we can love.

The regulative idea of approaching the whole can enable us to make some connection between love and justice, though since we are finite, conflicts between love and justice can always arise for us. (3) The universalising tendency *inherent* in reason – reason as a feature of our emotions – is not towards abstract universalising (the universality of the lowest common denominator) but towards the (necessarily limited) expansion of the circle of concrete particulars that we can love. This distinction between two kinds of universalising reason is of the first importance because the opposition to universalising reason is justified and not at all irrationalist so long as it is directed against abstracting from the concrete being of entities in order to say too little about too much. Such abstraction is characteristic of the use of statistics in the human sciences and concrete sciences generally, and even in management. It involves abstracting from many aspects of complex concrete beings in order to make them susceptible to mathematical calculation which can only take into account certain aspects of them. In this way reason transgresses the limits which human finitude imposes on it, and becomes fully universal, but at the expense of the loss of concreteness and qualitative knowledge. There are specific purposes for which it is legitimate to do so: justice, for instance. But because such abstract reason is necessarily truncated, justice cannot be the only moral value as Godwin thought, but must be tempered by mercy, and so on.

Finally, I want to return to the issue of head/heart dualism to ask how it can come about that Freud can be read as a head/heart dualist, and even drafted into the camp of 'pro-heart' irrationalism. A version of this dualist account of Freud can be seen in Timpanaro's book *The Freudian Slip*, where he attacks Freud for, among other things, presenting the unconscious as wiser than the conscious. Lacan presents a version of psychoanalysis which really does have this consequence.

Freud, as is well known, divided the soul into three agencies, the ego, the superego and the id (I follow the now familiar latinisms of the translators, though Freud's German words should have been translated 'I', 'over-I' and 'it'). To get a head/heart dualism out of this, one agency has to be got rid of. Both Timpanaro and Lacan effectively leave out the superego, transferring its properties to the ego, which hence becomes the repressing agency as well as the agency of reason, perception and action, as the ego was for Freud. For Timpanaro at least, the id is then lined up with nature, instinct or the biological, and the ego/superego with the demands of society for renunciation. But this is a mistake. The id is not, for Freud, the same thing as instinct, which is a border-concept between the psychic and the biological. Ego, superego and id are all psychological entities, not biological or social ones, though all three are produced in the first instance by the interaction of a biological organism with a socially structured world. All three – the nature of the id in any individual or culture, as much as that of the ego and superego – are social products; and all three remain aspects of a biological organism. This ought to be obvious – that the id is modified in its being by the socially structured repression which largely determines its contents, while the ego and superego too must have, or have had, biological functions. But by a fallacy of misplaced concreteness, it is often assumed that social being lodges uncontaminated in one part of the soul (and is social both in the sense of socially produced and socially functional, though these two things do not in reality always go together) while another part remains in a pre-social state of nature. Conflicts between biological needs and social norms are assumed to be reproduced neatly in the intra-psychic conflict between id and ego/superego, and the partisans of Nature and Convention take their sides. But the id is not like a virgin forest roamed by untamed beasts – more like an overgrown bombsite loaded with urban detritus and prowled by feral cats. It obeys the law of displacement because it is subject to repression; the aim of analysis – 'that there might be ego where there had been id' – is to undo repression thereby undoing displacement too, which is to say bringing what were parts of the id into the ego where they can be matched with their causes. The energy that had been bound up in the pursuit of unsatisfiable desires is thereby released for satisfiable ones. In this operation, one might say that the work of the ego and of the superego are diametrically opposed: the ego is reclaiming parts of the id for itself, the superego seeking to keep them split off from it and repressed.

I think this makes clear the essentially anti-therapeutic nature of Lacan's theory. Whereas for Freud wishes were displaced because they were repressed, for Lacan displacement is the essential nature of all desire. This makes all desire unsatisfiable, but the ruses of displacement by which wishes evade the censor are magnificent, even though this transformation means abandoning the goal of satisfaction.

There is a sense in which psychoanalysis can be said to be about the emancipation of the emotions from repression; but not their emancipation from reason. As Spinoza might have said, nothing can repress an emotion except another emotion. The emancipation of the emotions is simultaneously their becoming rational, by cause-object matching. 'Pro-heart dualism', which in a psychoanalytical context may be called pro-id or pro-unconscious dualism, is the defence of the repressed and displaced character of the emotions, rather as there are certain forms of 'workerism' and of feminism which aim, not at the emancipation of the working class or of women, but at the glorification of the qualities that they have as a result of being oppressed – hence the perpetuation of their oppression.

4 Beyond Spinozism
The objectivity of values

Now among those things which exist in any mode of being, and are distinct from God who made them, living things are ranked above inanimate objects; those which have the power of reproduction, or even the urge towards it, are superior to those who lack that impulse. Among living things, the sentient rank above the insensitive, and animals above trees. Among the sentient, the intelligent take precedence over the unthinking – men over cattle. Among the intelligent, immortal beings are higher than mortals, angels being higher than men.

This is the scale according to the order of nature; but there is another gradation which employs utility as the criterion of value. On this other scale we would put some inanimate things above some creatures of sense – so much so that if we had the power, we should be ready to remove these creatures from the world of nature, whether in ignorance of the place they occupy in it, or, though knowing that, still subordinating them to our convenience. For instance, would not anyone prefer to have food in his house, rather than mice, or money rather than fleas? ...

... Rational consideration decides on the position of each thing in the scale of importance, on its own merits, whereas need only thinks of its own interests.

(Augustine, *City of God*: book XI, ch. 16, pp. 447–448)

Augustine is certainly claiming here that the 'scale according to the order of nature' is the true scale in itself, and that insofar as we are rational, we recognise it. He obviously sees the destruction of species as a sign either of ignorance of their true place in nature, or as wanton selfishness. But he is not saying that we should never act in accordance with the order of utility. He is not saying that we should resign ourselves to having mice in the cupboard rather than cheese (this choice of example is no doubt light-hearted, yet a serious point is intended). As rational beings, we rank above mice, and may subject their interest to ours in certain ways, though we may not discount them. We should not kill animals for sport, but we may kill to eat, or – what is morally equivalent and could not be avoided even in a vegetarian world – to stop them eating our food.

Nevertheless, the higher standing of mice than cheese, or even of fleas than money, should mean something for us. If it does not, we are not exercising our own rational nature which is the source of our superiority, but are letting mere need or desire rule us as it does the beasts. For Spinoza on the other hand, the 'order of nature' appears to count for nothing. Even though 'in God' (i.e. even on the most materialist reading of Spinoza, in the real order of things) there is a conatus towards the persistence in being of mice, that is nothing to us. Yet we have seen that on Spinoza's interactionist model of our bodily being and its relation to the world about us, the conatus of other beings must count for something. After all, for Spinoza 'the more we understand singular things, the more we understand God' (Pt 5, prop. 24 in Spinoza 1985: 608), and joy and therefore love follow from such understanding.

The source of this paradox which so shocked Schopenhauer – that Spinoza the pantheist, the philosophical saint of all who love nature, took no account of animal welfare – lies in a tension which runs right through his ethical thinking. On the one hand, there is Spinoza the lover of understanding: the essence of the human mind is to understand clearly, it is this towards which our conatus drives us (thus described under the attribute of thought; under the attribute of extension this is a drive to interact more with more of nature, more effectively and sensitively). On this view, it is the truth of our ideas that is the good. To the extent that we have a genuine knowledge of what mice are in themselves, we will know that they are higher in the order of nature than cheese is; insofar as we rejoice in that understanding, we will love them in due measure – i.e. not as much as people, but more than cheese.

According to this tendency in Spinoza's thought (and it is the dominant tendency, as well as the nobler one) emotions are assessed by the adequacy of the ideas that they involve. A bad emotion is one based on falsehood. But alongside this, there is another criterion in Spinoza: good emotions bring joy, bad ones bring sorrow. Granted, Spinoza wants to show that these two criteria are equivalent, since joy is the perception of an increase in our powers (and hence our understanding) and sorrow a decrease in them; the understanding rejoices in its power to hold true ideas, and it holds false ones only insofar as it is subject to some external compulsion which can only be painful to it. But if it is true that understanding rejoices in the truth, it is only true other things being equal, as Spinoza seems to recognise in one place. A dedicated researching physician may well derive joy from discoveries he makes about the disease that is killing him, but it would not be unmixed joy. Some knowledge inevitably brings sorrow, and such sorrow can only be avoided by turning a blind eye to the knowledge. To do so would surely be rightly seen by Spinoza as intellectual cowardice, though there are those that would commend it as 'positive thinking'.

The idea that the 'wise man' should somehow be invulnerable to sorrow, through loving only what cannot be lost or not fretting about what is lost has a long history before Spinoza. Augustine criticises the Stoics in *City of*

God (book XIV, chs 8–9) for their doctrine of '*apatheia*'. He writes: 'if *apatheia* is the name of the state in which the mind cannot be touched by any emotion whatsoever, who would not judge this insensitivity to be the worst of moral defects?' (*City of God*: 564–565). The Stoics wanted to replace three of the four passions they list with rational emotions (*eupatheiai*) but for the fourth, grief or distress, they denied any place in the 'wise man'; both the idea of replacing passions with rational emotions and the exclusion of grief (in Spinoza's case, remorse and pity are excluded) look very like Spinoza. But Augustine comments that Christians 'feel fear and desire, pain and gladness in conformity with the holy Scriptures and sound doctrine; and because their love is right, all these feelings are right in them' (*City of God*: 561) Other-regarding emotions, even of the type that the Stoics deprecate, may be commendable too:

> Besides this, it is not only on their own account that the citizens [of the City of God] are moved by these feelings; they also feel pain on account of those whose liberation they desire, while they feel fear that they may perish; they feel pain if they do perish, and feel gladness if they are set free.
>
> (*City of God*: 562)

And he comments:

> If these emotions and feelings, that spring from love of the good and from holy charity, are to be called faults, then let us allow that real faults should be called virtues. But since these feelings are the consequence of right reason when they are exhibited in the proper situation, who would then venture to call them morbid or disordered passions?
>
> (*City of God*: 563)

The point then about painful emotions like fear or grief is not how painful they are but whether they are rightly directed.

> It comes to this then: we must lead a right life to reach the goal of a life of felicity; and this right kind of life exhibits all those emotions in the right way, and a misdirected life in a misdirected way.
>
> (*City of God*: 566)

He does not mince words about those who seek, not rightly directed emotions, but freedom from emotions:

> And if [the worldly city] has any citizens who give an appearance of controlling and in some way checking these emotions, they are so arrogant and pretentious in their irreligion that the swelling of their pride increases in exact proportion as their feeling of pain decreases. Some of

those people may display an empty complacency, the more monstrous for being so rare, which makes them so charmed with this achievement in themselves that they are not stirred or excited by emotions at all, not swayed or influenced by any feelings. If so, they rather lose every shred of humanity than achieve a true tranquillity. For hardness does not necessarily imply rectitude, and insensibility is not a guarantee of health.

(City of God: 566)

Do these strictures apply to Spinoza? Not I think to Spinoza insofar as he is faithful to what I have called the Spinozist paradigm. But what of his view that the rational person will not experience remorse or pity? Spinoza thought that a rational person would feel no pity, but would relieve suffering because of another kind of sympathy. But he thought that the person without *either* rational sympathy or pity would be worse than the person moved by pity, indeed 'inhuman'. I am inclined to agree, but with the proviso that since none of us is fully rational, no one can dispense with the safety-net of pity. In the case of remorse, of course a person who was fully rational in Spinoza's sense would feel no remorse, since they would do no wrong, but Spinoza is quite aware that this is not a possibility for us. An imperfectly rational person (and there aren't any others) will surely often benefit from remorse. The case is analogous to that of pity in that what is motivated by remorse – i.e. repentance – could also be motivated by rational grounds without remorse. But I am inclined to the view (*contra* Spinoza) that where a great evil has been done, there ought to be remorse as well as repentance. For 'under the aspect of eternity' the past is as much part of one's being as the present or the future, and to perceive one's past evil action without remorse is to misperceive it, i.e. to be affected by it with inappropriate emotion. Spinoza might reply that the right response to a past evil deed is repentance (which is forward-looking) but not remorse (which is backward looking). But suppose one had done a great harm by accident, through no fault of one's own. Repentance would be quite out of place, but not, I think, remorse. Remorse here is simply the recognition that one was in fact the cause of evil, experienced with the entirely appropriate feeling of sadness and regret.

The issue here is not entirely about what practical good will come of a feeling. C.S. Lewis says somewhere that we ought to be rejoicing whenever we are not repenting for a sin that we intend to immediately put right, or pitying another's suffering that we intend immediately to relieve. The trouble with this advice is that most of us have done harms that cannot be put right and continue to have effects; and we feel pity for too many people to be able to do anything about most of them. While we should certainly not wallow in such remorse and pity, not to feel it would, I think, be to misperceive the situation. The action *was* wrong, it *did* do harm, someone *is* suffering. The demands of understanding to recognise these truths conflict with the demands of 'positive thinking' to harden oneself by repressing awareness of them.

We must then decide between the central theme of Spinoza's *Ethics* – the cognitive paradigm – and the Stoic residues which it also contains. While accepting that knowledge brings its own joy to the understanding just by being knowledge, we must recognise too that it may also bring far greater sorrow, and should not be repressed on that account.

What follows if we take the cognitive option? If the cognitive paradigm is true, what makes an emotion appropriate or inappropriate is nothing self-referential about the person whose emotion it is, but the nature of the emotion's object. Appropriateness and inappropriateness are relations of emotion to object, analogous to truth, and dependent on the truth of the idea which the emotion involves. Fear involves the idea that the object is dangerous, and is appropriate if it is; love involves the idea that the loved object is good in some degree, and is appropriate if it is good in that degree. Just as to make sense of belief we have to recognise that it is the sort of thing that can be true or false, and which it is depends not on the belief or its holder, but on the object of the belief, so emotions aim at appropriateness to their objects, and miss their mark if the cognitive aspect – the belief – is false of its object.

With one reservation, this means that the quality of (for example) goodness must inhere in the object. The reservation is that the being of the object is partly relational, and it may be the relational properties that make the emotion appropriate to it, as well as the non-relational properties. Dangerousness, for instance, is clearly a relational property. (A Rhodesian Ridgeback, for instance, is dangerous to a strange person, but not to its owner, or to a tiger, or to a telegraph pole.) And among the relational properties will be relations of utility to the person who feels the emotion. Hence utility has its place, but only one place among others – it is one relational property that may justify emotive attitudes to the useful object, but not the only or the basic one.

But the case for the intrinsic value of things is not proved yet, for it might be only a fact about our emotions that they take things to be of intrinsic value; our emotions could be as I have described them without things having intrinsic value, that is, it could be just that we have emotions in a manner *as if* things had intrinsic value. No argument from the nature of our emotions, it might be said, could prove more than that.

The first step in replying to this objection is to point out that, when 'everything is as if' something were true, it is reasonable to assume it to be true unless we have some special reason not to. Have we got any special reason to assume that it is only 'as if' things had intrinsic worth? Such reasons might be that it makes no sense to talk about values independent of us, so our emotions *must* be interpreted on the 'as if' model; or that we have at our disposal evidence that throws doubt on the veracity of this appearance of our emotions. I have already argued in chapter 1 that we can make sense of things having value independently of our valuing them. But it might be claimed that we know enough about our emotions to know, not only *that* it will appear to us as if things had intrinsic value, but *why* it will so appear – and the explanation is all about us, not about the things. Rather as, when watching a film with a murder in it, we see everything as if the person is murdered, but we do not assume that anyone is, because we know about making films.

My answer to this depends on the fact that we can change our judgement about something's worth, and that when we do so, we are constrained to abandon the old judgement, because it has been shown to be wrong. There is an exact homology (which will turn out to be more than a homology) between my realism about worth, and realism in the theory of science and of knowledge generally. It is paradoxical that non-realism in the form of strong relativism in the theory of knowledge is largely a response to the facts of diversity and change in beliefs. Yet we cannot describe that diversity nor account for that change without assuming realism. For in order for two people or two communities to disagree, they must disagree *about* something. And in disagreeing, each is claiming that that which they disagree about is one way rather than another. If adherents of one view come to be convinced by the other then, assuming this to be rational convincement and not an outcome of mere propaganda, it will be because something about the object of their belief constrains them to change that belief. If for instance a Kuhnian paradigm shift takes place, that is because the earlier theory had accumulated anomalies in the process of trying to explain its object. Only because theories make this attempt do they accumulate anomalies and have to be replaced by less anomalous theories. If scientific theories were not attempts to explain aspects of the world that are themselves independent of the theories, they could never encounter unresolvable anomalies, and could maintain themselves in perpetuity.

What of changes in values then? The case is complicated by the fact that some changes in values do result from changes in society – in customs, social organisation or the technology used by society – and in such cases one is inclined to say: x was right in society s^1 (or at historical time t^1), but y is right in society s^2 (or at historical time t^2). Thrift may be a virtue in a capitalist society but not in a socialist one; courage in the military sense may be a virtue in a society where war is endemic but not in a society with stable peace, and so on. But in other cases, moral change can only be seen as reform or degeneration. If someone comes to regard factory farming as wrong and to insist on free range eggs only, that is not because technology or social organisation has changed, but because one has come to recognise the value of freedom for chickens. This involves the judgement that battery farming of chickens is wrong (or at least prima facie wrong) in any society. It is not just a question of 'seeing things differently' as in a gestalt switch. It is a question of having a better – more lively, fuller, more accurate – conception of what life in a battery does to a chicken. If one does not feel *constrained* by this conception, the belief is not a genuine moral belief. If someone says 'I will only eat free range eggs, but it's nothing to me whether you do or not', we can conclude that their aversion to battery eggs is prudential or aesthetic, not a moral aversion. A moral belief is experienced as objective, and a change of moral belief makes no sense unless constrained by its object.

Let me return for a minute to the debate between realism and relativism in the theory of knowledge. If we bracket off the fact that changes occur in beliefs (scientific revolutions, for instance) the argument that 'we can only know how the world seems to us, not how it is' seems to have some force, and agnosticism about the real nature of the world looks reasonable. But if we take as an example a change such as the discovery of oxygen and of the unreality of phlogiston, the contrast 'appearance/reality' no longer stands as a contrast between two simultaneous aspects of the world, to one of which we have access while we have none to the other; appearance has changed because we have found out more about reality. Or to take a non-scientific example, suppose I think that I can see a rabbit in a field, but when I get closer it turns out to be a bird; there is initially the possibility of making a contrast between the apparent-rabbit and the real-I-know-not-what; then the appearance gives way to truthful perception. The initial contrast is made at the time only if the judgement that it is a rabbit is tentative. Otherwise it is a retrospective judgement after seeing it fly off. Of course, discovery is never final because it is never complete. One may later find out all sorts of unsuspected things about the bird. But one will not discover that the creature which flew away into a tree leaving a few feathers behind as it did so was a rabbit after all. Moral change has the same structure of a move from appearance to a deeper, but always incomplete, knowledge of reality.

It will be asked: what reality does the moral reformer know better than those around him or her? There are three answers which are more familiar today than the idea that I am defending (that it is the same reality that is the object of ordinary, cognitive knowledge). Objective moral judgements have been thought to be about:

1   values, considered Platonistically as a separate order, distinct from the world of nature and society;
2   duties, objective claims on our obedience;
3   virtues, intrinsically good human qualities.

My defence of the objectivity of worth must not be confused with Platonism, which seems to me the least plausible of the three alternatives, for it requires some kind of supernatural moral sense with which to recognise the values. If the diversity of morals proves anything, surely it proves that we have no such sense. The account of values that I am defending places them not in another world, but in the beings that compose this world; being and good are convertible terms as Aquinas put it, that is, they have different meanings but refer to the same things.

The case for objective duties has an instructive history. Kant proclaimed it, the duties being eternal and, by the same token, too abstract to generate any plausible moral code. Hegel and (especially) Bradley made a strong enough case against Kant for culturally specific duties, different in different epochs and tied to the social structure of any time – a case which has been reproduced without their idealist metaphysics in 'communitarianism'. I rest my case against Kant on theirs. But even they have difficulty in accounting for the moral reformer. He or she appears as a law-breaker justified retrospectively by moral change. But in order to be a moral reformer, one must be convinced that there are values independent of 'my station and its duties' in terms of which these duties can be criticised. Duties, it seems, are culturally/historically relative, but there is something that is not, in terms of which they can be criticised.

Here I should perhaps clear up an apparent contradiction between this argument and some earlier writings of mine, particularly my book *Socialist Reasoning* (1990), and the essay 'Marxism and Universalism: Group Interests or a Shared World' (1992). Here I am defending objective worth in a strong sense: things have worth independently of us altogether. But elsewhere I have defended the view that, while there may be objective answers to moral questions in particular situations, these stem from the society to which the agents belong and the positions that they occupy in that society. So what is right or virtuous at one time may be wrong or vicious at another, and that for objective reasons, not just as a matter of different judgements. Of course *one* way in which moral change can occur is unproblematically compatible with my views about objective worth: since worth inheres in real beings, a change in the beings that there are changes the values that there are. But this is not the main source of moral change.

The issue is resolved in the following way: one can distinguish moral questions in a rather narrow sense – questions about *duties* – from axiological questions, questions about intrinsic worth. Questions of worth are in principle prior, since duties only exist so that there might be worth. Duties themselves have no intrinsic worth. Often they are intrinsically bad in that they are in some measure destructive of what has intrinsic worth, e.g. courageous actions endanger life, many duties inhibit and frustrate the desires (good in themselves) of the agents, just punishment causes suffering and so on. But they are duties because they are 'negations of negations', means of protecting or bringing into being some intrinsic worth whose existence is at stake.

Everything that exists has some measure of intrinsic worth, and this is independent of us; but the concrete duties that are generated by our general duty to love what has worth in proportion to its worth, vary immensely from society to society. And for quite objective reasons due to social or even technological change, old duties may become obsolete and new ones arise. It is easy to see how such developments as the welfare state, contraception or perpetual peace would abolish old duties (and perhaps inaugurate new ones).

Likewise, the emergence of the possibility of a classless society alters the nature of the duty to oppose oppression. None of this presupposes any change in the basic ontological hierarchy of objective worth.

Alongside moralities of duties and moralities of worth (or axiologies), there have been moralities of virtues (such as Aristotle's and Hume's) and moralities of emotions (such as Spinoza's, and arguably the New Testament's – by 'moralities of emotion' I mean moralities whose primary objects of assessment as good or bad are emotions). How do virtues (and emotions) fit into the picture that I have sketched? I think that some virtues have objective worth, while others do not, and that the latter may be historically transient. Virtually all of what have sometimes been called the non-moral virtues have intrinsic worth to some degree: intellectual virtues such as intelligence, rationality, foresight, perceptiveness, self-awareness, imaginativeness; social virtues such as politeness, wit, charm; physical virtues such as beauty, strength, fitness, dexterity. Some virtues generally regarded as moral which have an intellectual and social component are also, and pre-eminently, of intrinsic worth: kindness and truthfulness, for instance. But I am inclined to the view that the four classical virtues of courage, temperance, prudence and justice have value only as negations of certain negations that have prevailed in all societies hitherto, rather than intrinsic worth. And I am certain that ascetic virtues such as obedience, self-denial and sexual abstinence, have value only as negations of negations, and that their intrinsic worth is a negative one, i.e. they are bad in themselves. This does not of course mean that they are not sometimes necessary: they may negate much worse negations. But a society whose social order is such that they are rarely necessary is a better society than one in which they are often necessary. Emotions have intrinsic worth insofar as they are rightly ordered with respect to the intrinsic worth of their objects, loving beings in proportion to their worth. I have said enough about this since the morality of emotions was my starting point.

Where, then, is communitarianism right and where is it wrong? I have got three things to say about it.

(1) Communitarianism rightly opposes the idea of a Cartesian moral subject, abstracted from his or her social position. But it often tends to replace it with a collective subject which shares many of the features of the Cartesian individual subject. This holism is as mistaken a social ontology as the atomism that it attacks. Society is neither a bundle of separate individuals nor is it a collective subject or suprapersonal organism. It is a set of relations between individuals and their environment, relations which pre-exist any given individual, and partly constitute the character and the powers of the related individuals. Society exists: it is not a mere plural of 'person' (as 'army' has been said, absurdly enough, to be the plural of 'soldier'); but societies (plural) do not exist – nor does a Society (singular); 'society' is not a count-noun. Society is an open textured structure, without boundaries or corporate identity. 'Society does not consist of individuals, but

expresses the sum of interrelations, the relations within which these individuals stand' (Marx 1973: 265).

(2) The holism of some communitarians is an instance of a very common type of fallacious reasoning, of which I shall give three other examples to illustrate the structure. In each case, some form of atomism is rightly criticised and the essential interconnectedness of a group of phenomena is pointed out. But they are then accounted for entirely within the interconnected structure; the constraint of forces outside the structure are denied. Here are the examples:

(a) Sartre's conception of a person's fundamental project, in which all of an individual's motives and choices are essentially linked as aspects of a single choice of being. This conception enables Sartre to escape the absurdities of desiderative atomism, which empiricist theories of mind assume. But he will not allow that this total choice can receive motives from outside it (for instance from the individual's biological needs). Hence he arrives at his view that the fundamental choice is in each case an 'absurd', unmotivated choice.

(b) Kuhn's conception of a paradigm in the philosophy of science supersedes the old empiricist accounts of science as the cumulative collection of separate facts. A paradigm unifies a science and generates the details of its research project. But Kuhn then cuts off all connection between the paradigm and the aspect of nature that it seeks to explain. The object of a science is taken as internal to that science, making the growth of anomalies as a science progresses towards its crisis and paradigm-shift quite unintelligible, and preventing Kuhn from seeing that if science does progress, it progresses with respect to truth.

(c) The use that has been made of Saussure's theory of language, not indeed by Saussure himself, but by some of his structuralist and (especially) poststructuralist admirers. He rejects an atomistic model of language according to which each word is correlated with its meaning in a simple dyadic relation. Instead, he sees that a word is given its meaning by its relations to other words. But some have jumped to the conclusion that this means that language does not refer to anything outside itself, generating the characteristic linguistic idealism of the poststructuralists. They cannot conceive that language might refer *by virtue of* the relations between words, just as a map refers to the terrain by virtue of the relations between its symbols.

Communitarianism of the holistic type is another instance of this fallacy (let us call it the fallacy of the autonomy of wholes). Granted that the set of virtues and duties which constitutes the morality of any community forms a more or less coherent structure more or less suitable to the life of that community with its specific level of technology and its social order. But this set of historically changing and culturally relative duties and virtues is an attempt – more or less conscious, and more or less successful as the case may be – to grasp the objective value of being, which is itself partly independent of the society.

(3) Just as a scientific theory or paradigm always has specific historical origins and is only relatively true – it belongs to the transitive dimension of science – while that which it is about and which it tries to grasp cognitively (the intransitive object) is independent of it and explains the scientific changes that it constrains; so historical moralities are the transitive dimension of morality; its intransitive dimension is the intrinsic worth of beings, whether they are beings specific to a given society, or common to all societies, or independent of human society altogether: people and animals, buildings and plants, landscapes and heavenly bodies, mice and cheese and fleas and money.

Perhaps I should pause to comment here that the inclusion of human artefacts in this list of beings is entirely consistent with the thesis that I am defending, and indeed follows from it. I am arguing for the worth of all beings, independent of human valuations or utility; I am not arguing here for the special worth of those beings that 'come by nature', or are relatively unaffected by human action. I do not deny such special worth: I favour the letting-be of wilderness areas, and I regret the dumping of technological litter on the moon; I would mourn the demise of the dormouse, but welcome that of that obscene human creation, the oncomouse. But I do not argue for these positions in this book. The distinction between intrinsic worth and value as utility to humankind is not the same as that between natural and manufactured objects. A wind is a natural object, but can also have utility to us as power for our windmills – or disutility if it blows the roof off. A ruined abbey once had utility as a place for monks to live out their vocation, but still has value in itself – and not just as part of the heritage industry. Indeed, it follows from my thesis of the worth of being that even discarded lager cans and parts of cars have an intrinsic worth, though rather a low one, and much less than that of the woods and fields that they foul up. It is not possible anyway to draw a very sharp distinction between nature and artefact; if I want to be amid 'nature' I walk in the New Forest, but it only exists because King William the Bastard (alias the Conqueror) wanted somewhere to engage in cruel sports. (On the complex layering of the natural and the artificial, see Kate Soper's excellent book *What is Nature?*)

Of course, this objective worth of beings could not generate any morality unless there were some sort of ordering or hierarchy of beings, such as that proposed by Augustine in the passage quoted at the head of this chapter. The principle of ordering will be investigated in the following chapters.

5 Problems about the worth of being

I have arrived at an ethic or axiology which can broadly be called Augustinian, which I had adumbrated in the first chapter. It is an Augustinian ethic only in the sense of Augustine's theories of good and evil, not the nuts and bolts of his moral teaching, some of which is excellent, some of which is appalling, and all of which is conditioned by his time and place – a superficially Christianised Roman Empire, still founded on slavery, and threatened to its heart by barbarian attacks.

To recapitulate somewhat, the essence of Augustinian ethics can be summarised as follows:

1 All being as being is good:

> So we must conclude that if things are deprived of all good, they cease altogether to be; and this means that as long as they are, they are good.
>
> (*Confessions*: book VII, ch. 12, p. 148)

> all nature's substances are good, because they exist and therefore have their own mode and kind of being, and, in their fashion, a peace and harmony among themselves.
>
> (*City of God*: book XII, ch. 5, p. 476)

2 There is a hierarchy of beings. Those which have more being are greater goods than those which have less. 'To some [God] gave existence in a higher degree, to some in a lower, and thus he arranged a scale of existences of various natures' (*City of God*, book XII, ch. 2, p. 473). (See also the quote at the head of the last chapter.)

3 We ought to love all beings proportionately to their goodness – greater goods more and lesser goods less.

4 Evil is not being but privation or lack of being:

> evil things cannot exist without the good, since the natural entities in which evil exists are certainly good, in so far as they are natural. Furthermore, an evil is eradicated not by the removal of some natural

substance which had accrued to the original, or by the removal of any part of it, but by the healing and restoration of the original which had been corrupted and debased.

(City of God, book XIV, ch. 11, p. 569)

Compare Aquinas:

No being is said to be evil, considered as being, but only insofar as it lacks being. Thus a man is said to be evil, because he lacks the being of virtue; and an eye is said to be evil, because it lacks the power to see well.

(Summa Theologiae [ST] I, Q. 5, art. 3)

5   Evil comes from loving lesser goods more than greater. The love itself is not bad, for we should love all that exists. Only its reversal of the true *order* of goods is evil.

The will, however, commits sin when it turns away from immutable and common goods, toward its private good, either something external to itself or lower than itself.

(On Free Choice of the Will, book II, ch. 19, p. 82)

Greed, for example, is not something wrong with gold; the fault is with the man who perversely loves gold and for its sake abandons justice, which ought to be put beyond comparison above gold. ... anyone who perversely loves the goodness of any nature whatsoever, even if he obtains the enjoyment of it, becomes evil in the enjoyment of the good, and wretched in being deprived of a higher good.

(City of God, book XII, ch. 8, p. 480–481)

For Augustine himself, God obviously has most being and is therefore the greatest good; then people, then other sentient beings, then other living beings, then unliving material beings. But even the last category – rocks and rivers and stars – are good in some measure and have a corresponding claim on our love – see again the long passage quoted at the head of the last chapter. When he says 'Love and do as you will', Augustine can be read as saying 'Love everything in due order and do as you will.'

The hierarchy of being is further complicated for Augustine by two kinds of being that I have not reproduced in my lists. In the first place, he may have a Platonistic conception of some abstract values, and regard them as beings. Thus he says that the greedy person – perhaps a usurer or a corrupt judge – puts gold above *justice*, as if justice were a higher type of being. But this example can very easily be de-Platonised by saying that justice, while not a being but a set of rules, exists for the sake of people, and the greedy person is putting gold above people.

The second additional order of being is that of angels, which Augustine puts between God and people in his hierarchy. This could present an ad hominem problem for Augustine, since he also believes in fallen angels, which might be thought to have more being than humans but be less worthy of love. I suspect that Augustine would reply that the fallen angels are so corrupted by their fall that they have lost much of their being. 'Corruption' in Augustine always retains the sense of corrosion, rusting or rotting away, being deprived of some of the being proper to one. An evil being, in the moral sense of evil, is still good insofar as it is a being, and its evil is not only an evil will directed to other beings but a corruption of it itself, a loss of its being. This is the foundation of Augustine's teaching that we should hate the sin but love the sinner.

> further, since no one is evil by nature, but anyone who is evil is evil because of a perversion of nature, the man who lives by God's standards has a duty of 'perfect hatred' towards those who are evil; that is to say, he should not hate the person because of the fault, nor should he love the fault because of the person. He should hate the fault, but love the man. And when the fault has been cured there will remain only what he ought to love, nothing that he should hate.
>
> (*City of God*, book XIV, ch. 6, p. 556)

Anyway, so far as angels are concerned, Augustine concludes that:

> in establishing the order of rational beings, such weight is attached to the qualities of freedom and love, that although angels are superior to men in the order of nature, good men rank above the evil angels according to the criterion of righteousness.
>
> (*City of God*, book XI, ch. 16, p. 448)

However we can leave both Platonism and angelology aside without altering the core of Augustine's position. More serious is the question of his theological premisses. For Augustine himself, the goodness of being follows from the goodness of the Creator, and a properly ordered love of being follows from love of God taking precedence. For the purposes of the present book, I am setting aside theological premisses and trying to justify an ethic of the ordered love of being without appealing to them. The argument has been anthropological, even though the conclusion is not anthropocentric but ontocentric. In a sentence, it has been that we do not understand the good for humankind unless we understand that good is not derivative from humankind.

The Augustinian ethic so described will immediately arouse three objections, which it is the aim of this chapter to answer. First, it will be said that the idea that being is the good is a category mistake, for being is what is, while good refers to an end to be brought about. Second, it will be said that the fourth point listed above seems to say that evil is in some sense unreal: 'For you [God] evil does not exist, and not only for you but for the whole of your creation as well, because there is nothing outside it which could invade it and break down the order which you have imposed on it' (*Confessions*, book VII, ch. 13) – but isn't evil all too damned real? And third, it will be said that the idea of an ontological hierarchy is a non-starter because being is an all-or-nothing thing. One thing can be better than another, but not more existent. Hence Augustine's hierarchy of goods must be grounded in something other than ontology. I shall deal with these three objections in turn.

Good as being and good as end

One modern philosopher at least – namely Kant – has thought that at least one kind of being – rational beings – are ends in themselves. Kant too has been accused of a category mistake here.

> Kant distinguishes between independently subsisting and non-independently subsisting ends. This is forced upon him by the fact that he has already described man, i.e. all men, as ends. This, in the ordinary sense of the word, men are not. For an end is an object of desire, and an object of desire is something that does not yet exist. The notion of self-subsistent ends is nothing but an embarrassment to Kant.
>
> (Ross 1954: 51)

Of course there is a sense in which a person can indeed be the object of desire, and, if Sartre is right, that is not a mere elliptical way of saying that some act involving that person is an object of desire. But Ross's argument leaves it unclear whether a person cannot be an end because they exist while ends are not-yet-existent things, or whether no concrete object, past, present or future, can be an end. On the surface he seems to mean the former, but that surely cannot be right. We ought to desire a just society: that is quite independent of whether such a society already exists or is yet to be brought about. Ross presumably doesn't think that future people can be ends in themselves for us now, but existing people can't. Rather, the idea is that concrete entities can't be ends; this is quite a widespread assumption, with various abstract entities filling the role of end in various accounts – experiences, states of affairs, the truth of propositions – but it is no more than a prejudice. It is quite possible to hold both that good designates an end of a desire and that concrete beings are what is good. In Thomas Aquinas, for instance, in this matter as in many, Aristotle and Augustine are reconciled: good as end and good as being are fully integrated.

Goodness and being are really the same, and differ only in idea; which is clear from the following argument. The essence of goodness consists in this, that it is in some way desirable. Hence the Philosopher [Aristotle] says: *Goodness is what all desire*. Now it is clear that a thing is desirable only in so far as it is perfect, for all desire their own perfection. But everything is perfect in so far as it is actual. Therefore it is clear that a thing is perfect so far as it is being; for being is the actuality of every thing, as is clear from the foregoing. Hence it is clear that goodness and being are the same really. But goodness expresses the aspect of desirableness, which being does not express.

(ST I, Q. 5, art. 1)

Since goodness is that which all things desire, and since this has the aspect of an end, it is clear that goodness implies the aspect of an end.

(ST I, Q. 5, art. 4)

'Desire' here is *appetitus*: '*bonum est quod omnia appetunt*', '*bonum dicit rationem appetibilis, quam non dicit ens*'. Hence we are not only talking about conscious human desires, but about the tendencies of all things, for as a technical term in Aquinas *appetitus* is as near as may be to 'tendency' in modern philosophy of nature (for example, in Roy Bhaskar's critical realism). Thus Aquinas can say:

All things, by desiring their own perfection, desire God Himself, inasmuch as the perfections of all things are so many similitudes of the divine being ... . And so of those beings which desire God, some know Him as He is in Himself, and this is proper to a rational creature; others know some participation of His goodness, and this belongs to sensible knowledge; and others have a natural desire (*appetitum*) without knowledge, as being directed to their ends by a higher knower.

(ST I, Q. 6, art. 1)

The idea seems to be that everything has a tendency towards the actualisation of its own inherent potential, e.g. a tadpole has a tendency to become a frog. What is actualised is its being and is what its tendency is towards: the frog *is* a frog; and being a frog is the good towards which the tadpole had an *appetitus*, and presumably towards which the frog still has an *appetitus*. In the case of non-living beings, it might be said that they do not have any inherent *appetitus* to realise any hitherto unrealised potential, but they have an *appetitus* – or as Spinoza would say a conatus – to remain what they are: the structure of the rock is such that it tends to resist erosion, and so on. Although Aquinas talks in terms of ends and Spinoza denies that there are ends in nature, they are not so far apart as this would make them seem. The 'end' of a tendency is simply what it will lead to if unimpeded, and no tendency can be defined except in terms of such an 'end'. Those who find this way of talking about nature unacceptable as using an anthropomorphic metaphor should reflect that the medieval talk of ends in nature is no more metaphorical in origin, and rather less anthropomorphic, than modern talk of laws of nature. (Of course, the fact that something has a tendency does not mean that the tendency will be actualised. A tadpole may be eaten by a duck, a rock may erode away and so on. But all tendencies in nature are like this, since everything's conatus takes its chance against the conatus of other entities. 'Conatus' cannot be understood either as a literal 'striving', for only a living being can strive, nor as an inexorable tendency, but rather as a tendency in just that sense that bodies tend to remain at rest or in uniform motion in a given direction, though no body has ever actually so behaved.)

For Spinoza as for Aquinas everything has a tendency towards persistence in its being, but sentient and rational beings have a more complex tendency to fulfil their sentient or rational nature. We have seen that for Spinoza the human conatus is not just for the preservation of one's life, but for greater interaction/identity with more and more of being.

Both Aquinas's theory of *appetitus* and Spinoza's of conatus are theories of goodness for things in themselves rather than for us: the being of a rock is a good for the rock. When it comes to the idea of goodness *for us* the apparent conflict between good as being and good as end is disposed of in a different way by Augustine; but this argument presupposes that we have already established that things are good in a sense independent of us.

For Augustine good is not so much what is desired but what is to be loved. 'Love' here serves as a very general concept, including much weaker emotions than those commonly called love. To desire there corresponds an end, and the desire motivates the realisation of that end. To love there corresponds a loved being, and the love motivates a whole range of conduct towards that being, which conduct will of course differ vastly according to the nature of that loved being, but will often come under the rather Heideggerian headings of being-with, caring-for and letting-be. In the case of a rock, the appropriate conduct may be little more than abstaining from wanton destruction of it, and perhaps contemplating it aesthetically. As we go up the hierarchy of being, the sort of conduct motivated by love becomes correspondingly more complex and diversified.

Once it is accepted that the appropriate response to goodness is love (and to a given degree of goodness a corresponding degree of love), the problem about good as being and good as end really disappears. For love certainly takes beings, not events or facts or states of affairs, as its objects; it certainly motivates action; and it is quite naturally expressed by saying that for it the loved object is an end in itself.

However, this involves a paradigm of action different from that which has dominated modern thought. The model here is that one loves various beings in various degrees and conducts oneself towards them accordingly. Whereas for the dominant paradigm, concrete beings appear always as means to ends, and ends are specified more abstractly as events, experiences or states of affairs, and it is in these that the cycle of desire and action is completed. One feature of the dominance of this paradigm is that the climate of opinion has become increasingly hostile to the idea that anything at all could be an end in itself, since the abstract entities that feature as ends of one action get their value as means to another. The assumption which has come to dominate 'common sense' is that everything must have some purpose outside itself on pain of being 'useless'. In expounding Kant's ethics to students I find the difficult idea to get across is not just that people are ends in themselves, but that any ends in themselves could exist at all. And indeed, the university even requires that we specify the 'aims' of a philosophy degree. Kant and Heidegger stand out among the moderns in proclaiming that, in the one case, rational beings are ends in themselves, and in the other, all action terminates in a for-the-sake-of-which, which is always *Dasein* (humankind). But neither admit ends in entities outside humankind, despite Heidegger's ontocentric tendencies elsewhere in his work.

Yet it seems to me that Augustine's idea that a person's actions are motivated by their ordered series of loves for concrete beings, human or otherwise, is truer to human experience outside certain limited practices such as market-driven economic life which are arguably morally degenerate anyway.

The idea that the good resides in existing beings has a consequence that might be found objectionable from the standpoint of a certain kind of radicalism. One can imagine Sartre raising this objection. It is that this idea is inherently conservative. It places value on *existing* beings, not possible future ones. It involves loving beings for what they are, not for what they might be. This should not be exaggerated: the actualisation of a being's potentiality is part of its desired good. But it is the potentiality of an actually existing being, not a merely possible one. Likewise, knowing that posterity will actually exist, we have duties of care towards it; actual existence does not mean only what already exists. But we have duties to those who will exist, not to some ideal which might exist. We have no duty to try to bring about an ideal man or woman of the future, only to try to ensure that life is good for whatever men and women actually exist in the future. A certain type of utopian politics and moralism really is ruled out. I think that this degree of 'conservatism' should be accepted, as it was by Marx and Engels, whose fine passages of scorn for utopianism cannot be heeded too much.

There is another possible misunderstanding of the Augustinian position which needs to be cleared up here. Utilitarianism and the related ideal of 'economic rationality' have conspired to make many assume that whatever goal is recognised as the good should be 'maximised'. Are we advocating the maximisation of being? What indeed would that mean? In fact, there are rather few goods apart from money that it even makes sense to maximise, and ecologists have pointed out that maximising behaviour in general, as opposed to 'satisising' behaviour – seeking enough – is a source of danger to the environment (see Sylvan 1985).

We can perhaps imagine what it might be to maximise being by looking at Leibniz's conception of the goodness of God as consisting in his will to create the maximum compossibles, i.e. all the beings that he could create except those that would reduce the total variety of being. Crudely, if God did not create dragons, that is because they would have rendered more than one other species extinct by their voracity. But as soon as we transfer this notion of maximising being to the case of a finite being's activities it loses all sense; we can ask all sorts of questions about the effects of various courses of action, but not which would maximise being. We can only ask which would express the love of actual beings in a given order of priority. Love of being does not mean desiring that there should be as many beings as possible, it means cherishing existing beings and fostering the actualisation of their potentialities. As soon as the love of concrete beings replaces the utilisation of them for abstract ends, maximisation drops out of consideration altogether – and so much the better, for all maximising behaviour is irrational and destructive.

Deficient causes

> The truth is that one should not try to find an efficient cause for a wrong choice. It is not a matter of efficiency, but of deficiency; the evil will itself is not effective but defective. ... To try to discover the causes of such defection – deficient, not efficient causes – is like trying to see darkness or to hear silence. Yet we are familiar with darkness and silence, and we can only be aware of them by means of eyes and ears, but this is not by perception but by absence of perception.
>
> (Augustine, *City of God*, book XII, ch. 7, pp. 479–480)

The idea that evil is in some sense unreal seems to be common to pantheism such as Spinoza's and ethical monotheism such as Augustine's, for it seems to follow not from any denial of the autonomy of particulars, as is sometimes alleged in anti-pantheist polemics,[1] but from the idea that being as being is good, that is, from an idea that is common to Augustine, pantheism and the present book. Yet it is an undeniable empirical fact that a great deal of what goes on in the world is evil, and it is of the first moral importance that we identify this evil and struggle against it. Augustine himself, far from being oblivious to the evils in the world, was not only acutely aware of them, but also inclined to believe that evil generally prevailed over good in the world. Just as Kant described himself as an empirical realist but a transcendental idealist, one might describe Augustine as an empirical pessimist but a transcendental optimist. Is there a contradiction here – an internal contradiction in Augustine's thought but, if so, also an empirical refutation of the thesis I am arguing – or can the paradox be explained without contradiction?

One contention of this chapter is that Augustine and those that have followed him in this matter were not underestimating evil, but claiming that good is real in a sense in which evil is not, and indeed in a sense in which modern thought does not recognise either good or evil as being real. A further contention is that saying that evil is essentially negative is not the same as denying its reality (in some sense of reality).

Let us start by considering another philosopher who thought that evil is in some sense unreal, namely Spinoza. On the one hand, Spinoza's pantheism suggests that he would regard evil as lacking positive reality because all that is, is good. And I think this is one current in Spinoza's thought. Everything has a conatus, a tendency to persist in its being, and in that sense it can be said that for any being, its own existence is a good. All these conatuses exist in 'God or Nature', so for God or Nature the being of all that exists is good. This is the only sense which 'providence' can have for Spinoza, for whom there are no purposes in Nature. But insofar as human beings love 'God or Nature', they must inevitably take the being of all beings as a good. And I have already argued for a reading of Spinoza according to which, as our own being is perfected, so it comes to include the being of more and more things, and our conatus correspondingly becomes a conatus towards the being of more and more things, that is, we approximate closer and closer to (though still vastly distant from) taking the being of all things as our own good. The better people we are, the more we love all beings as goods.[2]

But there is another, more 'modern' side to Spinoza: according to this, the being of beings that are not 'like us', that is that are not human beings, is indifferent to us, and 'good' and 'evil' just mean conducive or adverse to our own advantage. On this view, evil is unreal in a sense, that is it is not objective – and good is unreal in exactly the same sense. This does not stop us truly calling things good or evil, because things really are conducive to or adverse to our advantage, and it is largely the same things that are conducive or adverse to the advantage of all who are 'like us'. Thus the subjectivist account of the meaning of 'good' and 'evil' does not lead to a subjectivistic ethics because human beings do not arbitrarily choose what to regard as good or evil, but will find much the same things good or evil. But it does lead to an anthropocentric ethics. On this reading, Spinoza is closer to Hume than to Augustine; Hume rightly rejects a particular attempt to explain away evil – that which treats particular evils as contributing to a better whole. But he rejects any idea that reason, in the broad sense in which it is concerned with matters of fact as well as relations of ideas, can recognise good and evil. They are recognised by sentiment, and sentiment is determined by considerations of utility or disutility to humankind. For Hume as for the 'modernist' side of Spinoza, a subjectivist account of the meaning of 'good' and 'evil' combines with a conception of the likeness of human beings and their mutual sympathy to generate an objective but anthropocentric ethics. Good and evil are alike unreal in the sense that they do not exist in the good and evil things themselves, but in the minds of the beholders. Good and evil are treated therefore as equally 'real' or equally 'unreal'. But this is not because Hume and the modernist Spinoza regard evil as more real than do Augustine and the pantheist Spinoza; it is because they regard good as less real. The difference can be shown schematically:

	Hume	Augustine
Being in itself	neutral	good
Being for us	good and evil	good and evil

Spinoza is with Augustine in his pantheist moods and with Hume in his modernist moods. Here we have the first distinction between Augustine and the moderns: not that Augustine denies the reality-for-us of evil, but that the moderns deny the reality-in-itself of good. Hence Augustine is not open to criticism from a modernist point of view for playing down evil.

But there is another difference between Augustine and the moderns. This is best illustrated by reference to another intermediate position, nearly contemporary with Spinoza's, and close to his pantheism; I refer to the position of the Ranters, a radical sect that arose in the wake of the victory of parliament in the English civil war, and the subsequent disappointment of radical hopes. Some at least of the Ranters seem to have held both that being as being is good, but that moral good and evil are dependent on our judging them to be so, and that such judging is a habit we should kick. Thus the Ranter Jacob Bauthumley tells us that, 'all things that God made were very good when he lookt upon them; But sinne God could not behold, because it was not' (in Smith 1983: 244). However when we treat sin as real, 'we call it and give it a being, though indeed in itself it hath none' (1983: 242).[3] Some Ranters used this idea to justify breaking the moral code of contemporary Puritanism out of which they had come. Thus Abiezer Coppe writes:

> Well! To the pure all things are pure. God has so cleared cursing, swearing, in some, that that which goes for swearing and cursing in them, is more glorious then praying and preaching in others.
> And what God has cleansed, call thou not uncleane.
>
> (1983: 92)

And most strikingly of all, another Ranter, Lawrence Clarkson recounts (1983: 180–181) that at one Ranter meeting:

> I pleaded the words of *Paul, That I know, and am perswaded by the Lord Jesus, that there was nothing unclean, but as man esteemed it,* unfolding that was intended all acts, as well as meats and drinks, and therefore till you can lie with all women as with one woman, and judge it not sin, you can

do nothing but sin: ... and Sarah Kullin being then present, did invite me to make trial of what I had expressed ...

– which they did.

This idea that acts, as being, are good in themselves, but are made bad by thinking them bad has such plausibility as it has in these instances due to the nature of the instances: the offence of swearing lies in the intention to offend, and to entice another to a sexual act which one believed wrong oneself would be objectionable even if the act would not have been wrong in itself. But it is noteworthy that the Ranters did not generalise this argument to cover murder or the oppression of the poor. Indeed, Coppe is very proud of his non-violence; after threatening the rich and mighty with 'levelling', he adds:

> Not by sword; we (holily) scorne to fight for any thing; we had as live be dead drunk every day of the weeke, and lye with whores i'th market place, and account these as good actions as taking the poore abused, enslaved ploughman's money from him (who is almost everywhere undone, and squeezed to death; and not so much as that plaguy, unsupportable, hellish burden, and oppression, of tythes taken off his shoulders, notwithstanding all his honesty, fidelity, Taxes, Freequarter, petitioning &c. for the same) we had rather starve, I say, then take away his money from him, for the killing of men.
>
> (Smith 1983: 89)

This combination of apparent amoralism which is however only applied to Puritan ethics, with non-violence and a communist social ethics, may attract the charge that the Ranters were moral reformers who mistook themselves for amoralists. However the Ranters did not see themselves as 'beyond good and evil' insofar as, like Augustine, they judged being as such to be good. While moral codes which deny this ontological good are rejected – including perhaps what I have called the moralistic paradigm of ethics – it may be supposed that the judgement that being as being is good had definite moral consequences for them, including the relief of poverty, as well as abstention from murder.[4] Their point is then a bit like Blake's when he says that vice is not an act but the hindering of an act in another (Blake 1966: 88). Indeed, it is also rather like Augustine's 'Love and do what you will', though of course Augustine did not draw the same scandalous conclusions.

Be that as it may, the Ranters' particular combination of an Augustinian teaching about the goodness of being with a modernist teaching about the subjectivity of judgements of evil is importantly different from Augustine's position, and not just in their iconoclastic approach to conventional morality. For the Ranters as for Hume and the modernist strand in Spinoza, evil is evil because we judge it so. Since good is good whether we judge it so or not, good is more real than evil; more real because more objective. For

Augustine too (as indeed for Blake) good is more real than evil, but not because it is more objective. Rather, it is because evil is essentially negative, and negative realities can only exist as negations (corruptions, diminutions) of positive realities. But negative realities are not just the shadow cast by negative judgements. They are as objective – as independent of our judgement – as positive realities, though parasitic on them.[5] There is a long-standing prejudice in the history of philosophy against the existence of negative realities – a prejudice of which perhaps Bhaskar's *Dialectic* has rung the death knell, if only enough people manage to read and understand it. Even Sartre, in whose system negative realities play a central part, treats them as mind-dependent. And the more obvious examples of negative realities do occur in the human world – Pierre's absence from the café in Sartre's own example, or such things as overdrafts or negative equity. Yet negative realities in nature too have effects, and having effects is the essential criterion of existence. The absence of rain causes certain plants to die and others to take over. This goes on quite independently of any judgements that we may make about it. It is instructive to look at the different use made of the example of sight impairment by Aquinas (in this matter an Augustinian) and Spinoza. For Aquinas (see above, p. 64) impairment of eyesight, being a lack, is an evil – not of course a moral evil, unless it is the effect of some human action or omission, but an evil nonetheless, which consequently we should take any acceptable opportunity to prevent or cure. For Spinoza we only regard blindness as evil because we compare it with sight. In themself, the blind person does not lack anything. But surely Aquinas is right here, for the human organism is so built that seeing is one of its functions. It is not designed to operate without sight. This judgement does not depend on any conception of the human organism as consciously designed or fulfilling a purpose; it depends only on the recognition that our organisms are wholes in which the different functions are interdependent. A blind person must take special steps to be able to function in a way that a sighted person can without taking such steps – that is why it is necessary to have special training schools, guide dogs and so on. Negative realities exist but they are dependent on positive realities for their existence (that, at least, Sartre got right). Blindness exists, but only because blind people and animals exist. One cannot call a non-existent person blind on the grounds that they can't see. A drought is a negative reality, but it presupposes a climate and eco-systems. The extinction of the moa is an evil and the threatened extinction of the panda is a threatened evil, but the non-existence of unicorns is not an evil. Here the version of the principle of plenitude held by Leibniz and Spinoza must be rejected. It is being, not possible being, that is convertible with good (unless possibility is taken as meaning the real potentiality of an existing being, as in existentialism).

Evil then really exists as a subclass of negative realities, which are all losses or absences or hinderings, etc. of positive beings.

Now it will be said, this is all very well in theory, but in fact many evils are perfectly positive realities. In particular it will be said that pain is as positive a reality as pleasure, and a false belief is as much of a belief as a true one.

It is indisputable that pain is as positive a *phenomenon* as pleasure. No one would mistake physical pain for absence of pleasure. Indeed pain, if not too severe, can coexist quite happily with pleasure. Pain has a feel all of its own, which is qualitatively different from anything else, and not the absence or negation of anything. But the same surely can be said of darkness. We are not only aware of darkness with our eyes, as Augustine says in the quote at the beginning of this section (p. 70), but from a purely phenomenological point of view, bracketing off what we know from science and attending only to our experience, it is clear enough that when we shut our eyes or when we open them on a starless night, we see darkness as surely as I can now, in broad daylight, see my bookcases and the mess on my desk. My eyes in darkness do not see nothing in the sense that my foot or the back of my head sees nothing. The visual field is there, but it is a dark field. Yet we are so convinced by the elementary scientific fact that darkness is only the absence of light that we are even prepared to tolerate teachers and lexicographers who give 'darkness visible' as an example of an oxymoron. The case of pain is similar. If, to speak Spinozistically, we look at pain under the attribute of extension, we see some threat or damage to an organism. Indeed for Spinoza mental pain too is a representation of some passing of the body from greater to lesser perfection. Naturally I am not concerned here with the neurophysiological definition of pain as C-fibres firing, but with a wider conception of the function of pain in the organism.

Something similar can be said with regard to false belief. A false belief does not have any inner mark to distinguish it from a true belief; it is just as positive a psychological phenomenon. It has causes and effects just as a true belief does. But if we consider belief under the attribute of extension, we see that true beliefs, insofar as they are not accidental but constitute knowledge, correspond to a high degree of interaction between the organism and its environment, the capacity to affect and be affected by many things in many ways. There is a real extension of the organism into the world underlying knowledge, which is lacking in the case of false belief. In view of this, I think it is legitimate to see false belief as a real lack, and not just a grammatical one – that is, it is not just that false belief can be truly described as lack of true belief, for after all true belief can be described as lack of false belief. The latter however is not a real lack. Negative judgements are always reversible; negative realities never are.

I have taken pain and false belief as about the most difficult cases in which to show that evils are negative realities. For many other ills – disabilities and frustrations of needs, death and other kinds of destruction – it hardly needs argument.

Degrees of being

Augustine's list at the head of the last chapter gives an intrinsically plausible account of the ontological order of the worth of beings. I do not hope to do more in this section than to spell out what is and what is not involved in that plausibility.

Augustine does not, so far as I know, give an explanation of this ordering in terms of any general principle. There are places where he does suggest some general principles for the ordering of values, but they are not ontological principles and they do not support the above list – than which they are indeed less plausible. Thus he claims that what is eternal is to be preferred to what is temporal, and that good that is common is to be preferred to good that is private.[6]

On the former: this serves Augustine mainly to distinguish love of God from love of creatures. It does not set up any ordering among natural beings – and it is just such an ordering that we are looking for here. It may be that he includes some Platonic ideas like justice and truth and beauty among the eternal things, but I don't think we should follow him there.

Furthermore his argument for valuing eternal things more than temporal things is questionable to say the least. It is a sort of utilitarian argument that if we value temporal things we can lose them and be plunged into misery, whereas if we value eternal things we can't lose them and are secure in our happiness. I don't think that this argument is really worthy of Augustine. It is reminiscent of the Stoics whom he criticises for their cold ideal of *apatheia*. Genuine love of a temporal being is always a risk, but a risk which it would be cowardice not to take. C.S. Lewis has some pertinent criticisms of Augustine on this issue in his book *The Four Loves* (1963: 110–112).

The idea of putting common good before private good has a pleasingly socialist sound to it. It does not in fact mean common good in the sense of goods which are communal possessions, but rather goods which are not owned at all, so that one person's possession of them does not exclude another's. Knowledge is such a good, since my knowledge does not reduce your knowledge, whereas material commodities are not such goods. This ideal of putting common goods in this sense first resembles Bertrand Russell's socialist ethic in his book *Political Ideals* (1963: 11 ff). But it does not differentiate natural beings as objects of different sorts of love, although it does differentiate different sorts of love for the same object – disinterested kinds from self-interested kinds, non-exclusive self-interested kinds from jealous kinds and so on.

But what is needed to justify Augustine's ordering of natural beings as flowing from the principle that being as being is good is some conception of different degrees of being, so that more being as more being is better. This idea is alien to modern philosophy which tends to define being in an all-or-nothing way: you can be or not be, but you can't be more or less. But this may be no more than an effect of taking the concept of being to belong to logic rather than to ontology: 'To be is to be the value of a bound variable' (Quine).[7] Yet just as there is a case for distinguishing negation as a logical property of negative judgements from real negative existence, so too by distinguishing an ontological from a logical sense of being and non-being, we may be able to make room for a conception of more or less being. In doing this I shall again be using Spinozist ideas, though for Spinoza himself, talk about more and less being can only have a rigorous sense in contrasting substance and modes, which is no more help to us here than Augustine's contrast of eternal and temporal. It is the sense of more or less being that Spinoza treats subjectivistically that I want to give objective content to here (see the preface to book 4 of the *Ethics*). To this end, I want to take up a usage of Tillich's, when he talks of 'the power of being' as something that a being can have more or less of.[8] That has more being which, in Spinoza's terms, has a more complex and articulated conatus towards being – which can more actively preserve and extend its being. This means interacting more with more of nature – the objective aspect of being more and more conscious. We humans interact more with more of nature than do non-human animals, which in turn interact more with more of nature than do plants, which interact more with more of nature than minerals, and so on. This seems like a basis for Augustine's ordering, and it is not absurd to call it having more or less being in the senses of extending one's being more or less beyond the boundaries of ones body in the narrow sense, and of projecting more explicitly the preservation and extension of one's being.

It is not the aim of this book to spell out the details of the ordering of beings and the ways in which those with more being take priority. There are many complex issues here, and there is an increasing body of work on them – with reference to animal rights, for instance. Here I shall limit myself to a few examples to forestall possible misunderstandings.

First, it should be clear from the fact that non-human and even non-living entities are good in the sense that I am using the word, that this sense is not the same as moral goodness. It could be called a pre-moral good in that morality is based on it. Morality presupposes ontological good and consists in loving it in due order, and – very largely – in fighting off threats to ontological good. Morality is for the most part the negation of the negation of ontological good. But moral good and evil may lead to an ordering of our sympathies which is not the same as the ontological ordering. For instance, I think it follows from this conception of good that to take pleasure in killing an animal is very morally bad. In the light of this, consider the anti fox-hunting slogan, 'Which animal in a red coat has your sympathy?' In one sense, of course the fox does: if it is within one's power to do so, one should enable it to escape. Yet if you have to choose between giving essential help to a seriously injured fox or to a seriously injured fox-hunter, you should without hesitation do the latter. That also follows from the ontological ordering of goods.

At the same time, this priority of humans over other animals does not mean that every time the interests of humans conflict with those of other animals the latter should be overridden. There is more to the ordering of beings as objects of love than the mere assignment of an ordinal number. There is a qualitative aspect to it. The sort of love that we ought to feel towards animals absolutely precludes torturing them or confining them in spaces where their natural movement is impossible, even if human interests in medicine or food would be served by such treatment. This qualitative aspect is precisely what would need to be spelt out in order to derive any concrete moral prescriptions from this theory of the good. But I shall have achieved enough in this book if I make it seem at all plausible that being as being is good and that the ordered love of being is the essence of ethics.

Problems about priorities also occur 'lower' down the ontological order. One objection that is sometimes raised against my position by environmentalists is that it would seem to override the protection of lower species from higher. If goats are eating a rare species of plant, the superiority of goats over plants in the ontological order would seem to preclude action to protect the plants at the goats' expense, unless of course the usefulness or aesthetic value of the plants to humans trumps the goats. But I would suggest that not only individuals but *species* and *eco-systems* have being and therefore worth, and may rank higher than individuals of a higher species. There is nothing in the Augustinian position itself that limits the being that has worth to concrete entities; as we have seen, for Augustine himself it covers Platonic forms such as justice, though I do not follow him here. My own Spinozist grounds for the Augustinian position might be thought to limit worth to concrete entities, but it also entails that eco-systems *are* concrete entities – composite individuals of a higher order than organisms, just as organisms are composite individuals of a higher order than cells. Species of course are not concrete entities, but they are nonetheless real, as having effects in the world of concrete entities. To spell out the implications of this would take me too far afield. I am concerned here to defend the general plausibility of the Augustinian ethic, not to work out its detailed application.

6 Away from anthropocentrism

Modern philosophy has until recently taken anthropocentricity for granted in ethics. It could hardly fail to do so because it has for the most part taken anthropocentricity for granted in ontology too. If being is no more than an ingredient of a human activity (knowledge), then it is no surprise if value is.

After Copernicus had shown that the earth wasn't the centre of the universe, modern philosophy soon retaliated by treating the human mind as the centre of knowable being. It has often been remarked that Kant's 'Copernican revolution' in philosophy was the opposite of the real Copernican revolution – and indeed Kant was only completing a counter-revolution that was implicit in modern philosophy from the outset. Modern anthropocentrism – so much more deeply anthropocentric than the mere cosmological geocentrism of the Middle Ages – starts with the epistemocentrism of Descartes. 'First philosophy' ceases to be metaphysics and becomes epistemology. Instead of asking about the place of humankind in the world as a condition of finding out how we know the world, knowing the world is first made problematic, and then the account of such knowing is made the foundation of the account of the world and our place in it. The epistemic fallacy – the transposition of questions about what there is into questions about what we can know – gives us an anthropocentric ontology. Our means of access to reality – at first conceived after Descartes as *ideas* – come to be seen as all we can know of reality. Yet the reverse is the case: we can only know ideas as the reflections of reality in us. They are further from us than the reality we know through them, as the window we look through is further from us than the scene we see through it. We can focus on the window only with difficulty and usually with small profit. We do not learn what ideas are until we already know quite a bit about reality, and then we learn about them by a process of abstraction (subtraction) from the reality that we know. And what applies to ideas (originally conceived from Descartes to Kant as determinations of consciousness) applies to other windows which more recent philosophy has come to regard as opaque such as language and practice. We learn language to talk about realities that have already been revealed to us in practice. And in practice, reality hits us in the face. If practice had been taken as the starting point of our knowledge instead of thought or sensation, modern philosophy could never have arrived at idealism. But once the pattern of idealist thought had caught on – the idea that we must first identify our means of access to reality and then conclude that we can't go beyond that means to reality itself – this pattern was applied to practice too.

Of course it may occasionally be useful to look at the windows: the study, for example, of the human eye. We may learn thereby about the limits of our vision: we can't see infra-red or ultra-violet light. But to learn how our knowledge is limited is not to learn that it is not really knowledge of the world 'out there', but rather to learn that there may be some things 'out there' that we can't know. If Kant had concluded, not that appearance is not of things in themselves, but that it is only of part of things in themselves, his argument would have been far less questionable. We know something, but not everything, about things in themselves.

Spinoza is alone among the immediate successors of Descartes in getting it more or less right. In the first place, he starts from ontology, not epistemology. He knows that we interact causally with our environment, and puts knowledge in its place as a presentation of the interaction. He knows that we know only aspects of nature in itself and that it infinitely transcends what we can know of it, but sees no reason to doubt that we can know those aspects adequately.

Even so, one feels that modern philosophy has a bad conscience about its non-realism. No idealist really succeeds in convincing us that they regard knowable reality as no more than an aspect of our knowledge of it. They combine idealism with 'empirical realism', which in effect means that they are realists outside the study. They play backgammon and exit by the door. And in every generation, there are those who see through the idealists' new clothes. But with non-realism about values it is not so. The idea that we put values there is the 'common sense' of the modern age, philosophical and unphilosophical alike. Doubtless this is to do with the turn in practical economic life away from the intrinsic value of things towards the exchange-value which their social relations confer on them.

The most promising new starts in the first half of the twentieth century were the parallel philosophies of John Macmurray and Martin Heidegger. Both started as they should from practice and the knowledge implicit in practice – which is knowledge of worth as well as of being. We have seen how Macmurray placed the capacity for objectivity at the heart of his account of human practice; rationality means relating to the true nature that beings have independently of us, and there is an emotional as well as a cognitive aspect to this relating; emotions can be appropriate or inappropriate to their objects. (Perhaps it is necessary to say that 'objectivity' here means existence independent of the subject. It is an opposite, not a correlative of 'subjectivity'. There is a tendency stemming from Heidegger to treat these terms as correlatives on etymological grounds, and use this verbal trick to tar those who are more realist than Heidegger with the brush of 'subjec-tivism', i.e. the doctrine of those who are less realist than Heidegger.) Heidegger defines humankind as Being-in-the-World, and shows that we are always already 'out there'. While he probably has etymological reasons for disliking the *word* 'realism' (thingism), he sides with realism in the 'doxographical' divide between realism and idealism (see *Being and Time*, 1967: 251), and presents a strongly 'anti-non-realist' position. Non-realism gets treated to what has seemed to some a Johnsonian, stone-kicking refuta-tion:[1] that we don't even know what we are ourselves aside from our worlds. Unless we presuppose a worldless subject which might question an 'external' world, proofs of such a world aren't needed and can't get started. The 'external world' is not external, not because it's 'in our minds', but because our minds are 'out there' in it. Insofar as idealism thinks that such proofs are needed and lacking, it is too wrong to argue with, so the attempt to provide such proofs is also a mistake. Yet of course the argument that this is so is itself a refutation of idealism.

But neither Macmurray nor Heidegger completely and consistently escape anthropocentrism. Macmurray, despite his rejection of epistemocen-trism, falls into the epistemic fallacy by thinking that primacy within practice means primacy in itself; thus, in an argument which I have criti-cised elsewhere (Collier 1994: 78–79) he concludes that causality only exists as an aspect of our agency, since we have knowledge of it only by abstraction from our practices. In another place, he argues that 'the mechanical' and 'the organic' cannot exist without 'the personal'. It is worth looking at part of this argument in more detail.

In *Interpreting the Universe*, Macmurray starts with a pragmatic account of science as an activity dominated by particular purposes, i.e. the manipula-tion of physical objects (1933: 85); hence the real is represented as stuff to be used. We are not interested in it for its own sake, only for its utility, and therefore for its causal properties (1933: 86). Science is a system of symbols representing general causal properties of things. It is therefore limited in point of view, though applicable to everything (1933: 87–88). It abstracts from individual properties to the extent of seeing things as identical units or series of units. It is concerned only with the number and order of those units. Hence it can be mathematical. Units differ only by their place in the spatio-temporal grid (1933: 92) and difference in space and time makes no difference to them. Here Macmurray thinks he has found a contradiction, but it is only an effect of his formulation of the problem, for while being located in a given place or time makes no difference to a unit, being related to other units in space or time does.

Now, however, we come to the main argument to show that the mechan-ical description of the world is inherently contradictory if regarded as a complete description. Any change in an arrangement of units must be caused by something outside that arrangement itself (1933: 95–96). Macmurray concludes:

> Since whatever is represented through the mathematical symbolism
> must have its activities referred beyond itself, it necessarily presupposes
> the existence of something which is not and cannot be represented in
> the symbolism.
>
> (1933: 97)

But this does not follow. Let us grant that any given mechanical system can
change only due to causes outside itself; but they can be causes located in
another mechanical system. Macmurray calls this an infinite regress, but it is
not a vicious regress. The chain of mechanical causes may extend forever
backwards. What Macmurray has given us here is quite simply the cosmological argument – Thomas Aquinas's Second Way – as a proof, not of God,
but of some non-mechanical cause. However it is no more valid as a proof of
a non-mechanical cause than as a proof of God.

The connections Macmurray draws between the utilitarian attitude to
nature as 'stuff' to be manipulated, mechanical materialism, and the mathe-
maticisation of nature is remarkably reminiscent of Heidegger, though as so
often Macmurray, by spelling out arguments which Heidegger has left us to
guess at, shows us his fallacies. This is entirely to Macmurray's credit.

Macmurray's aim here is to show that the mechanical description of the
universe *could not be* the whole story: it implies the organic or the personal,
and the organic can't be the whole story either, and implies the personal (see
the following chapter in *Interpreting the Universe*). Of course the mechanical
description *isn't* the whole story, but that is not the point. He is arguing for
the ontological priority of the personal over the mechanical (and the organic)
in the sense that the mechanical could not exist without the personal, since
to suppose it does generates a contradiction. Yet there was a time before life
existed, and mechanical laws operated then too – and another time when life
existed but people didn't.

Macmurray has arrived at an anthropocentric ontology, which is the more
striking as he did not start out from epistemology but from practice.

Yet Macmurray's argument merits a few more comments. He is
completely right in saying that mathematical thought and mechanism
abstract from and ignore many features of concrete reality. They ignore not
only the organic and the personal but the individuality, worth and qualitative character of inorganic beings, as Macmurray himself recognises. This
they do by virtue of their abstraction, which is in order for some, but not for
all purposes.

But Macmurray is not right about science in general. He tells us that 'all
science, so far as it is really science, rests upon the schematism of mathematical thought' (1933: 99). This is simply positivism with the value sign
changed. I don't think that even modern physics conforms to the model of
additive atomism depicted here, though Newtonian physics did. And there
are also concrete physical sciences like geology, besides organic sciences like
biology and sociology and personal sciences like psychoanalysis; Macmurray

seems to see such sciences as mechanical explanations within the framework of the organic (and possibly personal), but apart from biochemistry that account does not seem plausible. We need to recognise the existence and validity of non-mathematical, qualitative and concrete sciences. It is odd that Macmurray, who had some training in geography, and took Marx and Freud seriously, should reject this possibility. In fact the 'science' that conforms closest to Macmurray's model of additive atomism is neo-classical economics with its econometric pretensions. But of course the standing of this 'science' is contentious.

Heidegger, for all his cutting of the idealists' Gordian knot and his apparent ontocentricity, never entirely convinces us that his 'Being' doesn't mean something anthropocentric in the sense that it could not exist without *Dasein* (humankind). The talk about the history of being (an aspect of human history), and the fact that the ontology of *Dasein* is called 'fundamental ontology' should arouse our suspicion of an anthropocentric foundationalism parallel to (if infinitely preferable to) that of Descartes. Then there is the passage:

> Of course only as long as Dasein *is* (that is, only as long as an understanding of Being is ontically possible), 'is there' Being. When Dasein does not exist, 'independence' 'is' not either, nor 'is' the 'in-itself'. In such a case this sort of thing can neither be understood nor not understood. In such a case even entities within-the-world can neither be discovered nor lie hidden. *In such a case* it cannot be said that entities are, nor can it be said that they are not. But *now*, as long as there is an understanding of Being and therefore an understanding of presence-at-hand, it can indeed be said that *in this case* entities will continue to be.
>
> (1967: 255)

Let us not assume that Heidegger is making the silly mistake of confusing 'in such a case [i.e. if people did not exist] it cannot be said that entities are' with 'it cannot be said that in such a case entities are'. He does seem among other things to be making the trivial point that, whatever is true about being in the absence of people, nothing can be *said* about being in the absence of people, because only people talk. That is quite compatible with realism, though. But it is only entities, not Being, that he says will continue to be if people cease to exist, and he seems to be saying that there is only Being as long as there are people. I say 'seems', because he comments on this passage elsewhere. The phrase '"*is there*" Being' renders the German '*gibt es*'. While '*es gibt*' in ordinary German means 'there is', it could be read literally as 'it gives' and Heidegger favours this reading in his 'Letter on Humanism' (in *Basic Writings*, 1978). 'It means that only so long as the lighting of Being comes to pass does Being convey itself to man. ... The sentence does not say that Being is the product of man' (1978: 216).

This seems to mean that Being only gives itself to people as long as there are people for it to give itself to. But on the same page we are told that 'Being ... is the lighting itself' – and lighting surely is for Heidegger something that only happens in *Dasein*. So the question of Heidegger's anthropocentricity or ontocentricity is perhaps not conclusively decidable. It is certain that the influence of Heidegger has served to promote all sorts of pragmatism and even discursive idealism which are deeply anthropocentric. It is much less certain that Heidegger would have been pleased by that outcome. And it is also possible to retrieve the quasi-ethical aspect of Heidegger's *Being and Time* for an ontocentric outlook, as I shall argue in a supplementary essay to this book.

A route to realism which avoids any such lapse into pragmatist anthropocentricity has recently been found through the understanding of the sciences. In this area, Roy Bhaskar's researches are the most interesting. We have already seen the importance of his notion of explanatory critiques, both in refuting the idea that there is a logical gap between facts and values and in elucidating the method of Spinozist ethics. The Augustinian notion of being as good, and evil as a privation of being is also echoed in the view expressed in Bhaskar's *Dialectic* that every ill can be seen as an absenting. Here I am concerned with his move away from anthropocentrism.

Bhaskar argues that experiments are needed because the laws of nature do not exhibit themselves spontaneously in the course of events. We have to isolate particular causal mechanisms in closed systems in order to test these laws. Yet we *can* do this, and apply the laws discovered in this way in explaining what happens spontaneously in nature too. This shows that the mechanisms that we isolate in experiments are not mere human constructs, but are at work independently of us. Science goes beneath the surface that nature shows to everyday experience, and discovers deeper, underlying mechanisms. Furthermore, science doesn't rest content with the discovery of any given mechanism, but looks for deeper mechanisms underlying and explaining it. It is an unceasing process of digging deeper, uncovering previously hidden structures. Change in the state of any science is not typically either a slow process of accumulation of discrete bits of knowledge, or a sudden process of 'seeing things differently' on analogy with a gestalt switch. It is a process of uncovering previously unknown structures underlying and explaining known ones. The discoverable but inexhaustible depth of nature explains scientific change and progress. We cannot make sense of the way science develops unless we assume that these underlying levels are really there, independently of our knowledge of them. This independence is not just a matter of what would exist if there were no human beings, but of what existed when we did exist but had not yet discovered it, and what constrained the nature of our discovery to be this and not that. It is this constrained change of science that proves the action of an independent reality. A static science might be a mere human construct for all we knew, and a science which could be changed at will could hardly be anything else.

But science is in fact neither static nor changeable at will; it does change in ways constrained by its object.

If nature exists independently of our knowledge of it, then there is at least a chance that it has worth independently of our valuation of it. Realism about worth presupposes realism about being and is homologous with it. But it is not implied by it. At most, scientific realism suggests a homologous argument to the argument from scientific change: an argument from moral change to the reality of worth in being. Moral change does not consist in arbitrary leaps as Sartre thinks, nor is it always a response to changed circumstances. It is knowledge of the nature of animals that constrains us to abandon the ethic which permitted their unlimited exploitation. The conception of rationality that I developed in my exposition and critique of Spinoza is a conception of changing our emotions by virtue of increasing our knowledge of the objects of those emotions. It is a theory of worth that exists independently of us and that we can come to know; and it is also a theory of human beings as capable of becoming less anthropocentric, and as beings whose special destiny as rational beings is *not* to centre our values entirely on our own species. The 'proper study of mankind' is not just 'man', nor what is useful to 'man'. As rational beings, we can transcend the narrow limits of this humanism.

In addition to the potential support given by the realist theory of science to realism about worth (including non-anthropocentric worth), there has been a revival of belief in non-anthropocentric values in green politics and ecological philosophy. Indeed it is no accident that some of the best philosophical work on green issues comes from those with a realist epistemology and ontology much like the one I have defended. I refer to such books as John O'Neill's *Ecology, Policy and Politics* (1993) and Ted Benton's *Natural Relations* (1993).

But some ecological philosophers would regard the position I have defended as only non-anthropocentric in its meta-ethics, and as still perniciously anthropocentric in the content of its ethics. For like Augustine, I combine belief in values which owe nothing to humankind with belief in human superiority in a certain sense — or rather two distinct senses. According to Richard Sylvan's classification, this makes my position an intermediate one between shallow and deep ecology (see his paper 'A Critique of Deep Ecology', 1985). In what follows I hope to make clear what I do and do not hold on these issues.

In the first place, while recognising that beings other than human beings have some intrinsic value, I have also claimed that human beings have more value. I claim this not on the ground of loyalty to our own species, but on the ground that our species interacts more with more of nature than other species, or in other words is more conscious, rational and so on. This is my opinion and I am not going to retract it, but it is worth saying something about what its implications are. It implies that in addition to the duties that we owe to other species, we have special duties which we only owe to human beings. For instance we have the duty (other things being equal) to tell the truth to them. We could not of course have this duty towards other animals, let alone vegetables and minerals, not because of any quantitative precedence taken by humans, but simply by virtue of the nature of the species concerned. It is from the nature of the different species that different duties flow. Nevertheless, from the different nature of human and other animals' concern with the individual's possibilities, priorities of duty sometimes follow. When we have to choose between saving the life of a human and a non-human animal, we should choose the human. In this respect humans take precedence, but the scale of different duties to different species remains a qualitative not a purely quantitative one. It is because of the *nature* of sentient beings that we have a duty not to torture them, it has nothing to do with their *relation* to higher or lower beings. Hence it is not overridden by human interests. The hierarchy of beings is a hierarchy of complexity of natures, with different kinds of love and consequent obligations owed to each kind in virtue of their specific nature. It is not a pecking order.

But there is another way too in which the Augustinian position which I am defending might be regarded as anthropocentric. It takes it for granted that human beings are and will necessarily remain in some sense the rulers of the earth. Our rationality, i.e. our more effective and sensitive interaction with more of nature, means that we are in a position to make decisions for other species and kinds of being generally as well as for ourselves. In an ideal world (which of course is very far from our world), I believe that our rationality would actually make it suitable that we should rule other kinds of being, and Trotsky would be right to see the increase of our power over nature as a desideratum (but of course part of that power is the power to abstain from using our power, and in an ideal world that is a power we would use rather a lot). It is because and insofar as we are rational beings that it is appropriate for us to rule, for rationality is the non-anthropocentric principle within humankind. But whether that is so or not, it is clear that in the world as it is or as we could make it out of what it is, human powers have far more far-reaching effects on the earth than do the powers of any other species.

In what sense this amounts to ruling the earth is another matter. As things are at present, I think, only in the sense that a gang of bootboys sometimes claim in graffiti to 'rule London'. They certainly don't rule London in the sense that, for example, the Greater London Council used to rule London. Presumably they are claiming to terrorise London. And for the most part, humans terrorise and plunder the earth rather than ruling it in the sense of caring for it in accordance with an implementable plan. Short of collective suicide, we do not have the choice of ceasing to affect the earth profoundly by our actions. But we do have the choice of either planning our effects on the earth in such a way as to conserve its variety, complexity and fecundity – which might really be called ruling it – or on the other hand of letting the effects of our actions work planlessly. The tragedy of environmental destruction is largely what has been called 'the tragedy of the commons', though of course it is not the tragedy of what is communally owned, but of what is disowned. To avoid this, we have to take collective responsibility as a species for the future of the earth. We have to choose, not whether we will rule the earth, but in which sense: plundering and polluting and terrorising it, or planning for its future.

But of course ruling the earth in the planning sense is a much more conscious, organised activity than ruling it in the bootboy sense. It can only be done by those who actively intend to do it, and who have acquired the political power to do it. If we abstain from seeking to rule the earth, we will continue to rule it in the bootboy sense. For these really are the only alternatives. It is not just by being culpably careless that we damage the earth. So long as our interaction with nature is not carried out in accordance with a responsible plan, we will continue to damage it just by living. For instance, a common plan could organise public transport in sustainable ways. In the absence of a common plan, many are forced to own and use cars, polluting the environment and necessitating urban and rural destruction by road-building, and so on. The existence of such an anomalous entity as green car-stickers is witness to the compulsory character of environmental damage under planless conditions. For nothing that a private individual can do is more environmentally damaging than using a car, yet it is not hypocrisy but necessity that makes many sincere greens become motorists.

Before we can take ecologically responsible decisions, we have to have a mechanism in place for implementing those decisions; we have to have institutions empowered to plan the use and development of resources. Perhaps it will clarify matters if we distinguish two ways in which human power over the earth could be increased. By substituting common control for blind, market-driven blundering in our production of effects on the environment. And by developing technology so that our power (individual and collective) to produce effects is increased.[2] If the latter occurs without the former, we only become more dangerous bootboys. The former on the contrary increases our power over our power; our power to control the effects that we produce. Only this enables us to limit the effects of our powers. Under planless conditions, the increase of our powers to produce unplanned effects through technology inevitably proceeds. Indeed this productivist 'dynamism of the market' is the chief argument used against planning. But the market also determines how we use these powers, and it does so in a way that is indifferent to human and environmental damage done.

The aversion of many greens to the notion of humankind ruling the earth is reinforced by the ecological disasters of planning under state socialism. But in the first place, the claim for planning is not that it is a sufficient condition of ecological responsibility, only that it is a necessary condition of it. With planning, we can have either ecological care or ecological irresponsibility, according to whom we elect to do the planning. Without planning, we can only have ecological irresponsibility. In the second place, the

obsession with productivity under state socialism was an effect not of planning within nation-states, but of planlessness outside them. For these
nation-states were competing in the world market, and their productivism
like all unlimited productivism was market-driven. To a degree this was
inevitable. Even if they had chosen economic self-sufficiency, they were
under military threat, and could not arm themselves without industrial-
ising. When we consider the horrendous and inexcusable consequences of
Soviet industrialisation, both in human and in environmental terms, we
should also remember that this industrialisation was arguably a condition of
the defeat of Hitler.

For planning to constitute 'humankind ruling the earth', it could not be
confined within the limits of the nation-state. Much would need to be done
globally, and much locally; the nation-state should wither away in both
directions.

With these provisos, collective human control of our interaction with
nature at least enables us to respect the worth of non-human beings, even
though it does not by itself ensure that we do so (and neither does any other
institutional arrangement). It would for instance enable us to put a halt to
'progress' in any given direction that was deemed deleterious to natural or
human beings. So long as the free market rules our interaction with nature,
progress in production is literally unstoppable, however destructive its
direction.

The paradox has often been remarked on that many greens are hostile to
science, yet of all political projects the green one is most dependent on
scientific knowledge to show which policies are ecologically sound and
which are disastrous. It is a further paradox that greens have often
condemned human dominion, yet the establishment of that dominion in
place of the alienation of human powers in the market where they are uncon-
trollable is the first prerequisite of the green project's success.

Recent discussions of human power over nature seem always to interpret
'power' as an antagonistic relation, like the power of one class over another.
But the best model for power which involves care and precludes antagonism
is the power we have over our own bodies. Except for a sick asceticism, this
never means the power obtained by conflict and victory. We have power over
our bodies when we can run and play darts and see clearly, and we lack such
power to the extent that we are ill or unfit or clumsy. Nor is this the rule of
some other entity over our bodies; we are our bodies, and our rule is self
rule. And even if we sometimes care for our bodies in 'privative modes', by
letting them deteriorate, we never exercise power over them in the bootboy
sense of ruling. When Marx says that nature is humankind's inorganic body,
he implies that our rule over it should consist in caring for it, using it in a
way that preserves it, as we use our limbs and organs, not in a way that
destroys it, as we use a match. The proviso is necessary, though, that in
saying 'nature is humankind's inorganic body', we are not saying 'I will tell
you something about nature: it is our inorganic body.' That would be one

more form of anthropocentrism. Rather, we are saying: 'I will tell you something about humankind: nature is our inorganic body.' Just as, under the attribute of thought, our essence is reason, i.e. precisely the non-anthropocentric principle in us, so too, under the attribute of extension, our essence is to be constituted, not only by our bodies in the narrow sense, but by the larger organism consisting of their interaction with nature.

7 The worth of human beings

I have been defending a completely general thesis about being: that being as being is good (Augustine), or as the medievals put it, that the terms 'being' and 'good' are convertible. *One* consequence of this is that beings apart from human beings have intrinsic worth, and this is the consequence that goes against the grain of all post-medieval philosophy apart from recent ecophilosophy. It is therefore the part of my thesis that is likely to strike the reader most forcibly, leading to the misreading of my claim as one with relevance to one area of ethics only, environmental ethics.

But of course the Augustinian position that I am defending includes the idea that human beings have intrinsic worth, and indeed more intrinsic worth than other natural entities. I am proposing the worth of being as the 'intransitive dimension' of the whole of ethics, which every moral code approximates to more or less well, and under the constraints of its time-and-place-bound ideological determinants. One can be 'relativist' about concrete moral codes and theories, in the sense that Roy Bhaskar calls our scientific knowledge at any given place and time 'relative'. Yet just as scientific knowledge aims to discover a reality independent of it, and can therefore be more or less rational in its judgements, so moral codes and theories are shots at discovering real worth, and can be more or less rational as they do so better or worse. When criticising some prevalent moral idea, we must do so by appeal to the objective worth of beings. Ecological ethics gives striking illustrations of this; greater knowledge of animal ethology or of ecosystems or of crystal formations leads to the discovery of worth that we had not seen before, and consequently reveals to us new duties, virtues and vices. But most though not all ethics is concerned with how we should treat people. I have already defended here various theses about the worth of people that may have moral implications; that we are ends in ourselves, though not the only such ends; that we are at the top of the hierarchy of natural beings; that this position involves qualitative differences from, rather than quantitative priorities over, other beings; that our high position has to do with our ability to know and value beings other than ourselves; that insofar as our specific being involves the sensitivity to, and effectiveness of our interaction with, the rest of nature, we may achieve more or less of it, and so on.

What conclusions may we draw from this about the kind of ethics we need in our treatment of each other? What kind of care and what kind of justice will it lead to? Will it generate egalitarian conclusions (and if so which ones) or will it lead to a hierarchy within humankind, as part of the 'great chain of being' to which we belong? This chapter tries to answer some of these questions.

The first point is that the more clearly an ethic is based on loving each being in accordance with his/her/its own nature, the less it will consist of a set of rules, 'thou shalts' and 'thou shalt nots', of the sort that Kant thinks he can get out of his categorical imperative. Insofar as it includes such rules at all, they will belong to the obvious and uncontentious part of ethics, which no one apart from a criminal or a law enforcement officer is ever tempted to break, like the rules that we should abstain from torture and rape and wilfully killing innocent civilians. The main body of ethics cannot be formulated in such rules, but will consist in recognising the complexity and specificity of every individual being; each being should be loved in a different way, in accordance with its own nature. This is a great strength of the conception of ethics defended here. Moral codes which consist of do-s and don't-s serve mainly to excuse their adherents from thinking about how they should treat this particular being in this particular situation. They think that because they 'have observed these commandments from my youth up' (like the rich young ruler in the Gospel), they do not need to be sensitive to needs falling outside the scope of their list of rules, or even requiring breaches of those rules. It is quite possible to be a total swine to someone without ever breaking a universalisable rule in one's behaviour towards them, and most of the evils in the world, apart from those caused by politics and economics, are of this sort. Religious moralities are particularly prone to this sort of insensitivity, despite the fact that Christians at least ought to have been alerted to the matter by Jesus's strictures against the Pharisees. It is much more important, as well as more difficult, to be 'nice' than to be 'good', if by 'nice' we mean sensitive to the nature of other beings, human or otherwise, and so able and inclined to give them the appropriate sorts of love, and by 'good' we mean obedient to moral rules. Aside from those issues which can only be put right by politics, most human happiness and well-being depends on 'niceness', that is on whether people's behaviour and conversation confirms other people's being, for instance by showing gratitude for their company and attention to what they are communicating, or whether people undermine each other's being by impatient replies, fault-finding, put-downs and tangential responses. These issues, and not abstention from drunkenness or adultery or petty theft, are the 'weighty matters of the law'.

The second point is that a recognition that ethics aims (in theory) at the discovery of the intrinsic worth of beings and (in practice) at loving them accordingly, allows for quite a lot of pluralism about concrete moral codes – and that in three ways.

(1) Differences between different sets of virtues and duties may be entirely rational, since they may derive from the same ordered love of being under different material and social conditions. For in different kinds of society, appropriate to different stages of human history and even different geographical environments, different duties may need to be observed and, to an extent, different virtues cultivated. This kind of moral diversity is neither arbitrary nor a matter of one code being right and the other wrong, but a matter of different practices being the best way to love in one set of conditions from those that are best in another. A nomadic community will need a different family structure and different property rules from a settled one; the virtues of justice, generosity and hospitality will be very different in a society producing only enough for subsistence, a society with a limited surplus, and a society of abundance, and so on.

(2) Even within similar societies and within different subcultures of the same society, there may be different moral codes which are not intrinsically better or worse than each other, but which instantiate diverse though equally legitimate ways of expressing the love of beings. Diversity of lifestyles is (other things being equal) a good thing, like other forms of diversity, even though each lifestyle may entail its own values (duties, virtues and so on) incumbent upon its followers, and the values of one lifestyle may conflict with those of another. This sort of pluralism is perhaps particularly in place in the sphere of sexual ethics. However, while pluralism is to be welcomed (other things being equal) it should be recognised that it does create problems which require a special 'second-order' set of virtues in order that different lifestyles – even those that are equally good in themselves – can coexist without unwittingly wronging each other.

(3) But in addition to these two types of moral diversity, there is also the diversity which stems from the fact that some moral codes (or rather all to some – varying – extent) get it wrong about what has worth, just as scientific theories get it (more or less) wrong about what exists or has which causal powers. A theory which regards animals as machines and hence denies our responsibilities towards them, or a theory which treats human life and limbs (including health care, and indeed labour time) as saleable commodities is quite simply wrong, and needs to be fought against (by reasoning and, in some cases, by violence). Of course, one moral code may be better than another in some respects and worse in other respects. The medievals were better than modern liberals in treating ambition and 'economic rationality' (*pleonexia*) as vices, but worse than (some) modern liberals in accepting torture and the persecution of heretics. This is not a matter of different times and places or acceptable diversity, it is a matter of right or wrong, true or false. Indeed, one of Mill's arguments for pluralism and diversity is that one moral code may turn out to be better than another, and so teach humankind something. New lifestyles are seen as the moral equivalent of experiments. But this argument for pluralism would lose its point if diversity were always between equals. The point of experiment is to discover

something, to get closer to the truth. But where my account differs from Mill's is that I am claiming that progress in the knowledge of being and moral progress are not merely parallel; the latter presupposes and is rationally motivated by the former, in that it is only as we relate more to the real nature of beings that we can, or are inclined to, love them appropriately. Of course, not all knowledge is equal in its moral import; knowledge of ecosystems or of animal and human needs is much more salient than knowledge of sub-atomic particles or distant galaxies.

What sort of worth have human beings got? Our moral intuitions seem to conflict here: on the one hand we say things like 'all people have equal moral worth', and on the other we assess and rank people morally and in terms of all manner of powers and achievements. Are these two ways of talking compatible, and if so where should one end and the other begin?

In the first place, we have already distinguished the ontological worth of human beings from their moral goodness or badness. Obviously, mountains and rivers and woods can't be morally good or bad, and neither can animals, with the possible exception of a few higher mammals. So ontological goodness is not moral goodness, and the ontological worth that human beings have by nature is not dependent on their moral goodness. Indeed moral goodness presupposes ontological worth, since it consists in loving beings in accordance with that worth, and acting from this love. Moral evil consists in preferring lesser to greater ontological goods, and hence causing there to be more ontological evils (privations of being) than there would otherwise have been. And in certain respects we ought to treat people equally whatever their moral standing. The obligation to help a person who is injured or hungry for instance has nothing to do with their virtues or vices. Yet there are other ways in which one should obviously not treat good and bad people alike; if we do not encourage virtue and punish crime and oppression, there will be a lot more privations of being than there would otherwise have been. Indeed, moral evil does, according to Augustine, involve a loss of being on the part of the wrongdoer themself, an ontological loss, though without their ceasing to have the ontological status of a rational being deserving of the love appropriate to a rational being. We should therefore 'hate the sin but love the sinner'; if we restrict our love to good people, we become bad people, like the Pharisees in the New Testament, or even the 'incorruptible' Robespierre. We need to distinguish an all-or-nothing ontological worth (or metaphysical worth, as I shall sometimes call it) from a kind which can be lost or gained in various degrees.

I want first of all to discuss the sort of ontological worth which all people have equally, and the sort of justice which this worth entails. Then I shall discuss the sort of ontological worth (virtues) that humans have in different degrees, and the ways in which we should consequently be treated as unequal. Finally, I shall ask whether there is any tension between the human equalities and inequalities so defended.

At this point it is salutary to point out that one cannot be an egalitarian as such, just as one cannot be a nationalist as such; one can be a Welsh nationalist or a British nationalist or an Isle of Wight nationalist or a European nationalist, but not all of these things (though you can, like me, be no sort of nationalist at all). Likewise, you cannot be committed to every sort of equality, since some sorts are incompatible with others. As Marx says:

> Right by its very nature can consist only in the application of an equal standard; but unequal individuals (and they would not be different individuals if they were not unequal) are measurable only by an equal standard insofar as they are brought under an equal point of view, are taken from one definite side only, for instance, in the present case, are regarded only as workers and nothing more is seen in them, everything else being ignored. Furthermore, one worker is married, another not; one has more children than another, and so on and so forth. Thus with an equal performance of labour, and hence an equal share in the social consumption fund, one will in fact receive more than another, one will be richer than another, and so on. To avoid these defects, right instead of being equal would have to be unequal.
>
> ('Critique of the Gotha Programme', in Marx and Engels 1968: 324)

The last sentence is elliptical. What Marx is saying is that in order to avoid defects of inequality as consumers, workers would have to be unequal as workers, that is, not receive equal pay for equal work. Equality as workers means inequality as consumers and vice versa. Hence one cannot be an egalitarian about both things, any more than a Welsh nationalist and a British nationalist. It is interesting that Marx actually says that different individuals 'would not be different individuals if they were not unequal'. This is usually said by a rather silly sort of right-winger, meaning by it 'individuality would perish if privilege perished'. That of course is false; there can be any amount of differences between individuals without privileges being based on them, and indeed societies based on a high degree of privilege usually impose much stricter uniformity within each rank than relatively rankless societies would tolerate. But the point is that any difference between people, whether privileges are based on it or not, generates an ordering: people have unequally wide hips, live unequal distances from Knightsbridge and so on. But these orderings do not coincide. As soon as some ordering is made the basis for assigning relative claims on society's wealth, other orderings are ignored. We need some principle, which cannot be the principle of equality itself, for deciding which orderings are relevant. Marx is clearly committed (as the reference to 'defects' shows) to equal remuneration for equal needs, and consequently rejects (or assigns to a lower stage of historical development) equal pay for equal work. These are issues to which I will return, but my point here is simply that not all equalities are compatible, and so egalitarianism about one issue cannot commit one to egalitarianism about all issues.

The one great merit of Kant's moral philosophy (which is in other respects about my 'least favourite' moral philosophy) is his view that we are ends in ourselves; and the basis for this, our 'rational nature', is an all-or-nothing thing, not something about which there can be inequality between human beings. Even though Kant may have (as Hume certainly did) held racist views about intelligence, he held universalist and egalitarian views about our rational nature, and it was this that determined his attitude to intercontinental relations and his exemplary condemnation of imperialism:

> the inhospitable conduct of the civilised states of our continent, especially the commercial states, the injustice which they display in visiting foreign countries and peoples (which in their case is the same as conquering them) seems appallingly great. America, the negro countries, the Spice Islands, the Cape, etc. were looked upon at the time of their discovery as ownerless territories; for the native inhabitants were counted as nothing.
>
> ('Perpetual Peace', in Kant 1970: 106)

He gives China and Japan credit for seeing what had happened to these other countries, and having the sense to keep western traders out.

Yet Kant's 'rational nature' cannot be the all-or-nothing feature of human ontological worth that we want, since for Kant this rational nature is only one aspect among others of human nature, and the others are devalued by comparison with it. It is this that generates the sometimes quaint aspects of his detailed moral prescriptions; for instance his inclusion among 'perfect duties to oneself' not only abstention from suicide, but also abstention from 'self-stupefaction by immoderate quantities of food and liquor' and from 'wanton self-abuse'. He privileges 'mental pleasures' over 'physical pleasures' – a distinction that cannot even be made on the Spinozist account of human existence that I am defending here. Heidegger comes close to the formula we need for the ontological basis of metaphysical equality.[1] He says of *Dasein* (humankind):

> That Being which is an issue for this entity in its very Being, is in each case mine. Thus Dasein is never taken ontologically as an instance or special case of some genus of entities as things that are present-at-hand. To entities such as these, their Being is 'a matter of indifference'; or more precisely, they 'are' such that their Being can be neither a matter of indifference to them, nor the opposite. Because Dasein has in each case mineness [Jemeinigkeit], one must always use a personal pronoun when one addresses it: 'I am', 'you are'.
>
> (1967: 67–68)

Perhaps a similar point was being made by Colonel Rainborough in his argument for democracy at the Putney Debate of 1647:

For really I think that the poorest he that is in England hath a life to live, as the greatest he; and therefore truly, sir, I think it's clear, that every man that is to live under a government ought first by his own consent to put himself under that government.

(in Woodhouse 1986: 53)

– if we add, of course, that this applies to every she as well as every he.

This fundamental character of 'having a life to live'[2] seems to me to be the sort of all-or- nothing feature of human existence that we need, not only to define metaphysical equality but to justify material equality (just as Rainborough used it to justify electoral equality). For while 'having a life to live' is something that cannot be taken away except by death, living a life is not something inner, like Stoic freedom, it involves the need to have at one's disposal those material things which are requisite for life; it also involves the absence of the power of another to have one's own life at their disposal. By 'have one's life at their disposal', I don't just mean 'have the power to kill', but mainly 'have the power to determine how one should spend one's time', for time is what life consists of. Hence it seems to me that the metaphysical equality of having a life to live supports demands for material equality in two ways. In the first place, it requires that everyone should have a priority claim to certain necessities, overriding anyone's claim to have more than those necessities when these conflict. The list of necessities will include in the first place things without which one cannot have health, such as sufficient food, protection against the weather, an environment without harmful pollution, and access to medication when ill. Medical science can fill out the details of this list. Second, it will include things necessary for operating in the normal way for members of the particular society concerned. So in our society, the list would include access to means of education and transport.

In a world of great abundance, it would be possible to provide all these things for all, and still leave considerable wealth for some, and hence considerable inequality. In the actual world, providing these basic needs for all without depleting resources and storing up environmental disasters for the future would be difficult enough. But even if universal provision of basic needs were compatible with great inequality, the principle that everyone has a life to lead would not be. For most wealth does not consist in things that the individual owner can enjoy in isolation or in fellowship with friends or family. Most wealth takes forms that presuppose the non-existence of wealth for other people, and has no value unless others are poor enough to be dependent on the owner of the wealth. A great landowner is no better off than his neighbours if they all own as much land as they can work, and so will not work for him. In the post-war period it became a cliché that upper middle-class people were always saying 'You just can't get servants nowadays'. Their high incomes seemed of little avail if there was nobody whose domestic services they could buy with it. Likewise, there would be little point in the rich sending their children to public school if it were not the case that public school education gave *relative* advantages to its possessor over equally well qualified people with state school educations. And the economic dependence of one person on another, and the consequent power of one to have the other's time at their disposal, is incompatible with respect for the other's 'having a life to live'. Of course it is not incompatible with their having a life to live; that is a metaphysical given. Having a life to live is not annulled, but it is violated, by having one's time 'owned' by someone else. In one sense, however much an employer has paid for your time, it remains *your* time just as your ancestors do not become someone else's ancestors because he has bought their bones.[3] But the fact of having to live one's life as directed by another produces a permanent dissonance, a perpetual chafing of one's *jemeinigkeit*, as anyone who has ever worked in a factory or large office will confirm.

So each having a life to live requires not just freedom from absolute poverty, but freedom from that relative poverty which makes employment possible. It requires that everyone who is not the owner of their own individual means of labour should have an equal share in and right of access to some communally owned means of labour. In short it requires communism, with the proviso that, in economic life as in civic, government should be under the control of the governed.[4]

Now it might be said that there could still be considerable material inequality in a society based on common ownership and the prioritisation of basic needs. There could in fact be some such inequality, and it would not matter anything like as much as actually existing inequality does. But I think it unlikely that the inequality would be considerable. The idea that it would stems from the absurd notion that natural individual differences spontaneously give rise to great inequalities, so that constant intervention is required if this is to be prevented from happening. Of course, it is true that one artisan or small farmer, due to natural strength or skill, might produce twice as much as another and so have twice the income of the other. It is hard to believe that such differences could lead to ten times the income. And if land and labour-power are not saleable commodities, there is no way that the extra income could grow cumulatively. Once we pass from individual production to production involving the co-operation of many workers, it becomes transparently clear (what was less obviously true of individual commodity production) that work does not generate any natural individual 'entitlement'; the common product is common wealth to be distributed by common decision.

> Within the co-operative society based on common ownership of the means of production, the producers do not exchange their products; just as little does the labour employed on the products appear here *as the value* of these products, as a material property possessed by them, since now, in contrast to capitalist society, individual labour no longer exists in an indirect fashion but directly as a component part of the total

labour. The phrase 'proceeds of labour', objectionable also today on account of its ambiguity, thus loses all meaning.

('Critique of the Gotha Programme', in Marx and Engels 1968: 323)

The community might have various grounds for distributing wealth other than in accordance with the needs of its members. It might be necessary to pay more for certain work as an incentive for doing it. For this reason people in dangerous jobs such as fire-fighters, dirty ones such as sewer maintenance workers, boring ones such as supermarket cashiers or emotionally draining ones such as nurses, might get paid a little more than lawyers or scientists or university lecturers. This would be a matter of pragmatics, not justice. Justice, based on the principle that all equally have a life to live, demands only that all basic needs are met and that no wealth differences be great enough to allow one person to dispose of another's time.

Next I want to discuss two types of inequality between people which some people have recently wanted to deny on 'egalitarian' principles, though they do not follow from the metaphysical equality that I have defended, and are not necessary to the democratic communist society which I have suggested that metaphysical equality entails. Indeed, they are typical of a society radically alien to it.

They may be grouped under the title 'judgemental egalitarianism'. The first, which is the easier to make a case against, is the idea that two people's products are of equal worth, just because the two people are of equal metaphysical worth. There may be harmless instances of this, as when a teacher makes a principle of treating any two children's drawings as equally good. This can be regarded as a polite pretence, to be classed with a MPs calling their despised opponent 'my honourable friend', or the chair of a meeting announcing that some boring formality gives them very great pleasure. But a pretence it surely is, and this becomes obvious if we look at examples where something of practical importance hangs on the truth. A bridge which collapses is not as good as a bridge which sustains its intended use. The engineers who designed the respective bridges may be equally nice guys, and are certainly equally ends in themselves, but that is of no consequence. The product must be valued for what it is, not for who produced it. Likewise it is absurd to say that a symphony by Sibelius is of no greater value than the tooting of a child on a tin whistle, and anyone who did say so would be assumed to have a sad insensitivity to Sibelius's music rather than a deep commitment to human equality. Equality does not travel from person to work; neither does inequality travel from work to person. It would be monstrous to suggest that, if one had to choose between rescuing a great composer or a child from a fire, one should choose the great composer.

The non-travelling of equality or inequality from person to work or from work to person is easy to defend because the work, once produced, is independent of its producer. (Some) symphonies survive their composers, and (some) bridges survive their builders. But there are kinds of 'work' that are less independent of their producers: knowledge, for example. Yet in this case the knowledge has to be evaluated in terms of what it is about, not in terms of who has it. My opinion about sub-atomic particles is not as valuable as that of a physicist. Occasionally, this is explicitly denied. I recall a political education meeting of the Socialist Workers' Party, of which I was then a member, where one comrade who had lived in India and written a Ph.D. thesis about aspects of the Indian class structure, gave a talk about India. Afterwards, another comrade suggested that it was elitist to choose someone who knew about India to give the talk: any comrade could have given it. I am glad to say that this opinion did not prevail. But there is something similar in the idea of some sociologists of knowledge that since all people are equally rational beings, all opinions are equally rational. This rests on equivocation about the word 'rational'. 'Rational beings' can be an all-or-nothing metaphysical characterisation of human beings, as in Kant. In that sense we are all equally rational beings. But we are not all equally good at evaluating evidence or deducing conclusions, nor do we all have equal access to evidence. Hence some people's opinions about factual matters are worth more than others, and this in no way 'travels' to any judgement about the worth of the knower.

The reason why human metaphysical equality does not make us equal as cognitive authorities is that knowledge is *about* something, and is to be judged entirely with reference to what it is about. The judgement that one individual is a 'better' cognitive authority about some issue than another is not an evaluation of that person's worth but of their likelihood of getting it right about that issue. Of course, if like Berkeley and some postmodernists you deny that ideas have any reference, you cannot consistently make this distinction. But I will believe that someone really doesn't make this distinction when I see them go to an electrician to cure their bronchitis and a doctor to get their house rewired.

Now it might be said that, although not all factual opinions are equal, all evaluative opinions are. This could be defended by claiming that value-judgements don't tell you anything about what they refer to, they simply express their agents' attitudes. So, it might be claimed, there is nothing independent by which to judge their judgement, and so to assess the judgement is to assess the one who makes it. The idea that not all value judgements are equal might then be thought to 'travel' – to entail the denial of equal metaphysical worth – and it might be thought that for this reason upholders of metaphysical equality are committed to denying inequality of value judgements. But this is not so. Certainly it involves *some* sort of judgement of unequal worth, just as does the judgement that Stephen Hawking knows more about physics than I do. The latter is a judgement of cognitive reliability; the former a judgement of moral reliability. If I know that someone makes the value judgement that it is morally acceptable for the UK government to authorise the sale of instruments of torture to other governments, to send refugees back to countries where they are likely to be killed without trial, or to close hospital wards causing the avoidable deaths of children (all of which the Major government did), I will make a judgement about that person's moral reliability. I will call them a bastard. This will lead me to treat them differently in some ways from other people – that is, unequally. For instance, I would not vote for them, write them a character reference or invite them to a dinner party. But this moral inequality does not affect their metaphysical or material equality. Even a bastard has a life to live. Where it is a question of saving their life and limb, I ought to do so if I have the power.

I have argued in other places for the objective existence of values. My claim here is only that the inequality implied by saying that some value judgements are better than others is of the same order as other inequalities (such as those of knowledge and of the worth of people's products) which we must accept on pain of absurdity, and that this does not in any way impugn the metaphysical equality which is the ground for material equality. Of course it is open to anyone to use the word 'elitist' as a term of abuse for someone who holds that some opinions, factual and evaluative, are objectively better than others. In that case, I am an elitist and I think that everybody should be. Certainly, such elitism is in no way adverse to democratic and communist politics. Anyway, I frankly confess to the view that there is an objective hierarchy of values, implicating both ethics and aesthetics, and that a good society would be one that prioritised the higher values over the lower ones; and that this would involve such policies as promoting the integrity of the countryside by restricting motor traffic, and subsidising opera on the grounds that the best should be accessible to all.

Finally, I want to ask: are equalities of the sort that I have been defending (metaphysical and material equalities) and the sort that I have been attacking (judgemental equalities) actually mutually antagonistic, or just distinct? At the logical level, I think they are just distinct. It is perfectly consistent either to defend metaphysical and material equalities and reject judgemental equalities, as I do, or to make the opposite judgement, or to defend or reject all these forms of equality. But I think there may be a causal antagonism between them. In a sentence: metaphysical and material equalities are violated by the free market, judgemental equalities are generated by the free market. In a free market nothing (and therefore not human individuals) is an end in itself or has intrinsic worth. Having a life to live is of no account in the market; what matters is having marketable commodities or purchasing power. The market, as Marx and Engels say of the bourgeoisie, 'has resolved personal worth into exchange value' (1968: 38).

It is also quite clear that the free market is incompatible with material equality. It invariably aggravates existing inequalities and adds new ones by the large element of chance that it involves, and by the way it favours the unscrupulous and those to whom money is the only value. Every freeing of the market, within or between nations, has led to greater material inequalities, including absolute poverty even in the world's richest nations.

At the same time, the market has its own kind of egalitarianism. It does not care who or what you are, only whether you've got money or saleable goods. It doesn't care what you sell, as long as it does sell. It doesn't care what beliefs and values underlie your desires, as long as those desires are backed by purchasing power. Of course, this is 'inegalitarian' in that desires backed by no purchasing power are 'ineffective demand' and are systematically ignored, and desires which cannot be commodified are discriminated against. TV watching and motoring require marketable commodities and are therefore promoted; conversation and love of nature do not, and so are pushed aside. But no desire is judged intrinsically worthy or unworthy, no value intrinsically bad or good or better. Profit being equal, pushpin is as good as poetry. It is surely this levelling of all values and the associated quantitative reduction of all qualitative distinctions and alienation of all personal agency into an impersonal market force, rather than any social egalitarianism, that the existentialists have denounced as 'the levelling process' (Kierkegaard) or the power of 'Das Man' (Heidegger).

Yet the market's indifference to intrinsic values is sometimes praised for its anti-elitism. It promotes popular culture rather than elite culture (how could it not? – popular culture was purpose-built for it). It has an apparent ideological neutrality which looks fair as between all cultural differences (even though it has always existed in symbiosis with racism). It does not matter whether you are humanist, Christian or Muslim, it will still sell you electric batons for torturing your political opponents. It does generate a certain degree of social mobility denied by more traditional class systems, and the consequent rise of the occasional person of lowly origins to a position where they can cheat and oppress their former peers looks egalitarian to those who think that equality of opportunity is important. It is presumably this sort of egalitarianism that John Major was appealing to when he promised a classless society while presiding over the growth of material inequality in the UK to its highest level this century.

As Marx pointed out (see p. 94) every equality means that unequal individuals are viewed from one side only; in the free market, people are viewed as agents of effective demand: any unit of effective demand is equal to any other unit. Given the inequality of effective demand, this is radically incompatible with material equality. But it requires judgemental equality, for as soon as one postulates an objective hierarchy of values, one calls into question the legitimacy of treating all effective demand as equal. So the free market is not after all ideologically neutral. It has its own ideology: judgemental egalitarianism.

The discussion of judgemental inequality has already touched on the question of virtues and vices. For though bad judgement does not diminish a person's metaphysical worth as one who has a life to live, it does diminish their moral standing. All virtues involve (relatively) true opinions and all vices involve (relatively) false opinions, as I have argued earlier. Of course, opinions about different things are involved in different virtues and vices:

one may be a great scientist but a lousy husband, or vice versa. But true opinions are just as much involved in being a good husband or a good friend as in being a good scientist, for it involves the cognitive virtues that I have discussed earlier such as sensitivity, perceptiveness, thoughtfulness, sincerity and so on. And these virtues – indeed virtues generally – are, like all cognitive achievements when considered under both attributes, matters of ontological ranking, though they do not affect the metaphysical equality of status as beings with a life to live.

The nature of this ontological ranking follows from the Spinozist account of moral worth defended earlier. Both between levels of being and within them, the basis of the ranking is more or less powers of interaction with other beings, powers 'to affect and be affected by' more of nature. This greater or lesser ontological 'perfection' involves both a greater or lesser capacity for love of other beings, and greater or lesser claims on particular kinds of love. Although this is a single scale, it involves dialectical 'qualitative leaps' such as that between humans who have a life to live and other animals which, while they live, do not 'have a life to live', that is to say, being is not an issue for them as it is for us. But within humankind, there is inequality in this degree of interaction, both between people and between different times in a person's life. Virtues are powers of greater interaction, vices lacks of such powers. It is possible analytically to distinguish effectiveness (powers to affect more of nature more) from sensitivity (powers to be affected more by more of nature). Nevertheless in reality these always presuppose each other. In order to bring about effects, we need to be aware of what we are affecting and the process by which we affect it; in order to increase our awareness of beings, we need to be able to actively uncover them, by heightened perceptiveness or by experiment.

This account of virtues and vices means that we must include in the list of virtues, not only qualities related to sensitivity such as I discussed earlier in my defence of the cognitive character of virtues, but effective powers, 'Nietzschean virtues', which are commonly excluded from the list of moral virtues: intellectual virtues, and physical virtues such as strength, skill, dexterity, health, fitness, beauty. (Of course, even the distinction between intellectual and physical virtues is not tenable in the last analysis if we accept a Spinozist philosophy of mind, and indeed it is not clear which group sharp senses or a good memory or even 'empathy' would fall in.) There seem to be two related but distinct reasons why these are often not regarded as virtues in the full sense (aside from the claim that they are trivial, to which I shall return): first, because they are not things that everyone can have just by willing to have them, and there is a Kantian strain in our ethical thinking which tells us that 'ought implies can' and that qualities the lack of which cannot be remedied by choosing them cannot have moral worth. This seems to me to be an example of the wrong sort of egalitarianism, the sort that thinks that the equal metaphysical worth of having a life to live leads to some sort of moral equality (though in this case only an equality of moral opportunity, not of moral attainment). I can see no reason to accept it.

The second reason, which is easily confused with the first, is that it is thought that what cannot be had by willing it is not changeable by us, so that to value it cannot motivate action, and is therefore morally redundant. But this is certainly not so. Though the intellectual and physical virtues cannot be had just by willing them and cannot be had by everyone in the same degree, they can be promoted by care for ourselves and others, and by institutions that foster them – or conversely diminished or destroyed by lack of such care and such institutions. And in case these virtues still seem trivial to some, consider how unhappy a community would be where they were lacking – and the fact that some puritanical communities which have devalued them relative to the 'moral' virtues really have been such unhappy communities. Of course Kant himself, having exiled the intellectual and physical virtues from ethics by his doctrine of the good will, recalls some of them by his claim that we all have a duty to cultivate out talents. However, his dualist account of our rational nature and his ill-informed remarks about South Sea islanders suggest that he would not include talents for darts, joke-telling, rock and roll or sexual intercourse in the list of those we are obliged to cultivate.

One more unusual feature of this account of virtues is that there can, in a certain sense, be exosomatic virtues. We can affect and be affected by more of nature in more ways because of our access to tools and telescopes and microscopes and tape recorders and hearing aids. 'Virtue is knowledge', but knowledge is stored in libraries and computers and videos and calculators as well as in human brains. If intelligence is a virtue, then 'artificial intelli-gence' is also a virtue – but always a virtue of some (usually human) animal which uses the computer or whatever, not of the computer itself. I am much more mathematically intelligent because I have got a pocket calculator than I could ever be without it. But if life ceased to exist, intelligence would cease to exist, however many calculators, computers and robots were left littering the landscape. So virtues may be exosomatic in the sense that the entity which corresponds to them under the attribute of extension may not be part of any biological organism; but like other virtues, they can only exist as the quality of some biological organism.

To summarise: (1) there is a metaphysical equality of worth of all human beings as 'having a life to live' independent of the various intellectual, phys-ical or moral qualities of the person. This is the foundation of the virtue of social justice, which requires stricter material equality than any literate society has hitherto practised, though perhaps some (ancient Israel, Russia under Lenin) have aspired to it.

(2) Nevertheless the virtues, which are cognitive and physical powers and liabilities, are unequally distributed, and it is important that we value these and do not blind ourselves to excellence in them by inappropriately extending our idea of equality to our judgements about them.

(3) Neither are all virtues equally important. Every virtue involves being able to affect and be affected by more things in more ways, and the more we interact with beings the more we love them. But the worth of different beings is different, and their claims on our love more or less; therefore different spheres of interaction generate differently valued virtues. It is after all better to be a good friend than a good physicist, and it is better to be kind to animals than to be good at producing marketable cosmetics.

Supplementary essay
Authentic existence and the fullness of being

In this essay I want to defend the existentialist notion of authenticity or authentic existence as an aspect of the good for humankind. I shall not discuss the various critiques of this notion, which I think rest on misunderstandings. I shall mainly be engaged in a fairly free interpretation of Heidegger, which I hope will forestall these misunderstandings. (To anticipate, one of my aims will be to show that if authenticity ranks among the virtues, it is not a 'self-regarding virtue'.) But it is worth saying first that the often-heard criticism to the effect that one might be authentic yet evil is hardly to the point, since (1) one may also be courageous and evil, prudent and evil, conscientious and evil; that is no argument against courage or prudence or conscientiousness; (2) the typical status assigned to authenticity is not so much either *a* virtue or *the* virtue, but that without which all virtues are just splendid vices; (3) existentialists *have* given us reason to believe that *certain* evils are inconsistent with authenticity: manipulative relations with others, according to Heidegger, anti-Semitism (and presumably racism in general) according to Sartre, sexism according to Simone de Beauvoir.

The concepts of authenticity and inauthenticity are introduced by Heidegger (1967: 68) directly after Dasein[1] has been characterised as (a) in each case mine, and (b) having Being as an issue for it. (Though Heidegger also says it is *my* being which is an issue for me, he has initially said, not my being, but Being. Cf. Sartre: 'we could apply to consciousness the definition which Heidegger reserves for Dasein and say that it is a being such that in its being, its being is in question. But it would be necessary to complete the definition and formulate it more like this: *consciousness is a being such that in its being, its being is in question insofar as this being implies a being other than itself*', 1957b: lxii.) *Mineness* is clearly seen as essential to our non-thing-like status: 'Because Dasein has *in each case mineness* [*Jemeinigkeit*], one must always use a *personal* pronoun when one addresses it: 'I am', 'you are'.' (1957b: 68). That I am a 'who' not a 'what' is the basis of my human dignity. At the same time, because (my) being is delivered over to me to be 'an issue', it can be won or lost. If won, it is authentic, 'that is, something of its own' (1957b: 68) if lost, inauthentic. But even if lost, (my) being is not like that of a log or a logarithm, to which 'mineness' does not apply. We must have mineness to be inauthentic, just as our being moral beings is a necessary condition of our being immoral, our being rational beings is a necessary condition of our being irrational, and so forth. Many Heideggerian concepts work like this. A positive designation is given to an *existentiale* which may nevertheless often exist in a deficient or privative mode: letting things go to pot is a mode of concern, not giving a damn is a mode of solicitude, and so on. Mineness is the condition of the possibility of authenticity and inauthenticity alike; at the same time, it does, I think, indicate that authenticity has a certain priority, just as rationality has priority over irrationality in that irrationality can only occur as a defect in a rational being. Inauthenticity may prevail in that 'in the first place and for the most part' we are all inauthentic, yet as beings characterised by mineness, we are all, so to speak, destined for authenticity, and could not be called inauthentic if we were not.

The definition of authenticity recalls the German root of the word *'eigentlichkeit'*, 'ownedness'. This suggests that authenticity means *avowing* as opposed to disavowing (one's) being – though not in the shallow sense in which avowing and disavowing are performatives, but such that one's whole life is an avowal or disavowal. Inauthenticity is 'washing one's hands' of one's acts, *ponziopilatismo*, as Gramsci called it.

After these preliminary remarks, I turn to (1) the role of the authenticity/inauthenticity distinction in Heidegger's account of what it is to be a Dasein (1967: ch. 1.4), (2) authentic and inauthentic 'understanding' (ch. 1.5) and (3) conscience as attesting the possibility of authenticity (ch. 2.2).

I

When Heidegger raises the 'existential question of the "who" of Dasein' (1967: 150), Anglophone philosophers are apt to think that this is a case of 'language going on holiday': we understand the question 'Who?' as a request for the name of someone identified ostensively or by description, or as a request for ostensive or descriptive identification of someone named. It does not seem to make sense to ask 'Who is humankind?', or, except in special circumstances, 'Who am I?' Yet in its place in *Being and Time*, this question expresses a real problem which has arisen in the development of Heidegger's notion of Dasein as Being-in-the-World.

The problem is this: throughout Heidegger's analysis of Dasein as Being-in-the-World, his fire is directed against conceptions of people as *substances*, whether physical or spiritual, or any Cartesian mismatch of the two. But if we are not substances, what are we? Not Humean bundles or Kantian noumena, that's for sure.

> But if the Self is conceived 'only' as a way of Being of this entity, this seems tantamount to volatilizing the real 'core' of Dasein. Any appre-

hensiveness however which one may have about this gets its nourish-
ment from the perverse assumption that the entity in question has at
bottom the kind of Being which belongs to something present-at-hand,
even if one is far from attributing to it the solidity of an occurrent
corporeal Thing. Yet man's *'substance'* is not spirit as a synthesis of soul
and body; it is rather *existence*.

(1967: 153)

But we need a more concrete account of personal identity, or as Heidegger
prefers to say 'self-constancy', before we are convinced. And Heidegger gives
us not one, but *two* such accounts: the self-constancy of the 'they' (inauthentic existence), and that of resoluteness (authentic existence). Insofar as I
am one of the 'they', I share *their* self-constancy, the predictability of what
'one must do'. Insofar as I have taken hold of my own existence, I have the
self-constancy of resoluteness.

So when Heidegger asks 'Who is Dasein?', he is asking 'How do we have
self-constancy without substantiality?', and when he tells us that in the first
place and for the most part we are the they-self, he is answering that such
constancy is provided by the tyranny of the disowned consensus that
'prescribes the kind of Being of everydayness' (1967: 164). Perhaps it still
needs to be said that this protest against the 'they' is *not* any of the following
three things: (a) a plea for the 'exceptional individual' against 'the masses': it
is under the 'dictatorship of the "they"' that 'we shrink back from the "great
mass" as *they* shrink back' (1967: 164); this shrinking is one more expression
of inauthenticity – Heidegger is not Nietzsche; or (b) any sort of 'abstract
individualism': we are not inherently 'individuals' who may or may not have
been able to resist 'conditioning'; rather, we are instances of the 'they', who
may or may not have been able to assume responsibility for our originally
disowned being. Nor (c) is it a matter of 'doing your own thing', 'doing it
my way' as against considering the views of others concretely. For the
'others' that constitute the 'they' are 'not definite others' (1967: 164), and
include oneself: 'one belongs to the others oneself and enhances their power'
(1967: 164). The distinction is rather between an up-front decision, whether
taken individually or collectively, off one's own bat or on the initiative of
definite others, as against the case in which the 'they':

> can be answerable for everything most easily, because it is not someone
> who needs to vouch for anything. It 'was' always the 'they' who did it,
> and yet it can be said that it has been 'no one'. In Dasein's everydayness
> the agency through which most things come about is one of which we
> must say that 'it was no one'.

(1967: 165)

This account is reinforced by Heidegger's account of language. Because
we necessarily learn language from others, without necessarily having any

personal acquaintance with the things to which language refers, we are initially in the position of blind people using colour-words. Afterwards, this can be corrected. The alienation that comes with language is necessarily prior to authentic use of language, but of course it does not rule out the latter. Heidegger is not a poststructuralist; both the dispersedness of the self and the disrelation between language and the world are features of inauthentic existence, not of human existence as such.

II

Understanding is one of the fundamental concepts, the *existentialia*, of Heidegger's 'existential analytic', which correspond in the world of human existence to the *categories* of Kant's transcendental analytic, applicable to the world of things. Coming in a triad with *state of mind* and *discourse*, *understanding* represents our cognitive being, as (analytically) distinguished from our affective being, *state of mind*. They are only analytically distinct, not really separate: every understanding comes with its own state of mind and vice versa. Understanding is not primarily *theoretical* cognition – it is after all analytically distinct from discourse. It is the understanding implicit in any practice, like Macmurray's 'knowledge' which is prior to 'thought', since in order to spell things out and criticise them in thought, one must first have a store of implicit knowledge, 'in a practical state' (as Althusser would say), acquired just by living. We may call understanding 'cognitive', even though Heidegger tends to use 'knowledge' only for theoretical knowledge. Understanding includes the various forms of 'sight' such as *umsicht*, the circumspection which informs our practical concerns and *rücksicht*, the considerateness by which (if mostly in deficient and privative modes) we acknowledge the being of others.

Understanding is characterised by the projection of some possibility of being, which lights up the instruments for, obstacles to and routes towards that possibility. We understand things in terms of their usability as part of a series of instruments gathered into an 'equipmental totality' by the projection of the possibility of Dasein towards which they are instruments. We may imagine a torch shone on the place we are going to, which also laterally lights up the things to be encountered on the way. We make projects in the everyday course of living, and our worlds are organised around these projects, as intricate networks of means for, hindrances to and backcloths of these projects. We *understand* the things in the world as to-hand for the sake of the projected possibility. This structure of worldhood has already been described by Heidegger (1967: ch. 1.3). What is new here is the focusing on the cognitive aspect, the *disclosedness* of the world, and the claim that this disclosedness comes with the projection of some possibility of Being. Understanding is always understanding of a 'for-the-sake-of-which', that is, of a possibility for the sake of which we are engaged in that world; and things within that world are understood as for the sake of that possibility ('things', that is, insofar as they are to-hand, not merely at-hand. Heidegger does not think that things exist for our sakes, but they are *primarily encountered*, and necessarily so, as to-hand rather than at-hand).

Now we come to the possibilities of authenticity and inauthenticity with regard to understanding. Understanding always has two aspects: the possibility projected and the involvement with the world. But it can be 'diverted into', or 'devote itself primarily to' one or other aspect (1967: 186). If the possibility of being is foregrounded, we have authentic understanding; if the world is foregrounded, we have inauthentic understanding. Let us consider some concrete examples.

On three occasions I have worked, for periods of two and a half to three months each time, as a hospital porter. In the first of these hospitals, a local geriatric one, the Management Committee came to look around while I was there. It was deemed untidy to have dirty plates around in the wards, so the patients had to go without food until well after their normal meal-time. The hospital, it seemed, must run smoothly despite the patients; indeed, it would doubtless have run much better if there were no patients at all. The second hospital – a world-famous London teaching hospital – provided even more striking instances. On one occasion another young and inexperienced porter and I were sent to take a 'bed' from one ward to another. 'Bed', of course, refers to a patient in a bed. 'Beds' were normally only taken when the patient could not be transferred from bed to trolley and trolley to bed again. When we arrived at the 'bed's' destination, the sister snapped at us 'I'm not having that bed in *my* ward!' Once convinced that the paperwork was in order, though, she realised that she had to accept the patient, but insisted that we transfer him from one bed to another. The patient was greatly overweight, and had an intravenous drip on one arm. The sister stood and watched grumpily, hands on hips, while we – no muscle-men – did our best to move the patient without hurting him. Fortunately a passing nurse, uninstructed by the sister, noticed that a third person was needed to hold the drip-pole, and did so. Seeing our difficulty in lifting the patient, the sister commented 'I don't want him dropped on my floor.' On another occasion, those porters not off on jobs were sent off on the entirely useless assignment of arranging chairs in straight lines, so that there should be no apparently 'unemployed' porters around – and no one to deal with an emergency should one occur.

The project of the hospital was of course the care of sick people. To that end, the smooth running of 'equipmental totalities' is required, and to that end disciplined functional hierarchies – administrators, doctors, nurses, porters – are set up. The focus moves away from the patients, towards the equipment, its smooth running, adherence to rules and respect for hierarchies designed to secure that smooth running. In the end, the tail wags the dog, the equipment to-hand wags the Dasein. One more anecdote: on night shift, we often had to sit with attempted suicides, to make sure they didn't repeat the attempt. The night sister would do her rounds, flinging the door open and saying 'And how are you?', closing the door again before you could look her in the eye. Maybe she had a big round to do, and could only complete it if she behaved in this manner. But for what? 'She doesn't care how I am' said one patient, and I had to agree.

Three points could be made about these examples, two of them political: (1) more funding for hospitals could give staff more time to relate humanly to patients. That is true. But the temptation to slide into servicing the equipment to-hand rather than the possibilities of Dasein would not go away. We have all heard the plea of social democratic politicians: '*First* we must raise productivity, *then* we can improve social services'; consider how this plea is endlessly repeated, irrespective of the level of productivity reached. (2) Before working in hospitals, while I advocated workers' control of nationalised industries, I made exceptions in cases like hospitals, since here the interests of the workers should be entirely subordinated to those of the patients. They should of course – but the worst way to do so is to subordinate the workers to hierarchies of command. It is just those hierarchies which obstruct human relations between workers and patients. When such relations occur, they occur *despite* the 'machine'. Workers' control of hospitals could only make them better places for patients by removing the pressure from above to put the smooth running of the machine before the needs of the patients. But it is no panacea. Whatever the form of organisation, these two possibilities – entanglement in the world of our practical concern, projection of possibilities of Dasein's being – are present. Hence we need (3) a constant readiness to break free of our equipmental entanglements and make straight for the possibilities of Dasein, for the sake of which that equipment exists. This does not mean, of course, that 'we can do without equipment, we only need goodwill'. We cannot serve the possibilities of Dasein without servicing equipment. But situations do arise where we must choose: it has been ironically suggested that, in the parable of the Good Samaritan, the priest and Levite may have been on their way to a meeting of the Committee for Safe Travel on the Jericho Road.

To further illustrate this non-political aspect, which I am claiming is an instance of the distinction between authentic and inauthentic understanding, let us consider the example of a relationship of love between two people. I am aware that such relationships can also be the sites of oppression, but what I am going to talk about has nothing to do with such oppression.

Perhaps the most usual way for love to turn cold is that the lovers come to be absorbed in the practical details of their life together – the housework, repairs, money matters. Attention to all these is necessary, and may be motivated entirely by the desire for the good of the relationship. But they easily come to obscure that aim, and the little conflicts about how to stack the dishes or which household expenses to curtail come to loom larger than the love. If a new love looks more promising than the old, it may be precisely because it is the project of love that looms large in it – it has not yet got a 'world' to get entangled in. If any love is to survive, it is necessary that sometimes the 'world' should disappear, outshone by the love that has brought that 'world' into being as a set of practical demands and equipment to be serviced. In this situation too, a temptation parallel to the social democrat's economics presents itself: 'if only we could get the daily routine problems solved, behind us, out of the way – then we could concentrate on each other again'. So the effort to solve them is redoubled, as if they could ever be 'got out of the way', and the entanglement is worsened.

Now I want to discuss a rather different case, to illustrate another aspect of the ethics of 'worldly entanglements'. My attention was drawn to this case while trying to answer, in my lectures on existentialism, the accusation that authenticity is an excuse for evildoing; often, Heidegger's involvement with the Nazis in 1933 is cited in this connection, and Sartre's fine political record is held to be anomalous – as the inconsistency of a man who is better than his philosophy.

I turned to some lectures given by the theologian Rudolf Bultmann during the Nazi period. Bultmann was a close friend of Heidegger's when they were at Marburg (i.e. while *Being and Time* was being written), and while Bultmann is commonly regarded as a disciple of Heidegger, the influence was probably two-way. By his own account, Bultmann was not a political person. His attitude to politics is a Lutheran one: the state is a necessary evil in this evil world, and we should submit to it as a Christian duty. He nevertheless became a member of the Confessing Church, which refused to collaborate with Nazism, and his brother died in a concentration camp.

In lectures given during the Nazi period, Bultmann clearly took his distance from Nazism. To someone raised in a more activist tradition of Christianity (such as the English 'Nonconformist conscience'), and with the benefit of hindsight, his criticisms of Nazism may seem naive and inadequate, or even as 'praising it with faint damns'. But at the time it must have taken both moral courage to depart from Lutheran acquiescence, however reservedly, and also of course physical courage to risk the wrath of a regime that lived by terror.

A few of Bultmann's criticisms are of specific aspects of Nazi politics: the practice of denunciations, the defamation of Jews. Incongruously but symptomatically conjoined with these two horrors is – the re-naming of streets! This is significant, because the underlying charge against Nazism is its *idolatry*, of which all these other wrongs are seen as symptoms. The state and the nation are seen as part of the created world, ordained by God, but not to be worshipped. Bultmann's favourite biblical text is quoted:

I mean, brethren, the appointed time has grown very short; from now on let those who have wives live as though they had none, and those who mourn as though they were not mourning, and those who rejoice as though they were not rejoicing, and those who buy as though they had

no goods, and those who deal with the world as though they had no
dealings with it. For the form of this world is passing away.

(1 Cor. 7, 29–31, Revised Standard Version)

Does this cut any ice against Nazism? Yes, I think it does. At first sight
it may seem not to, in that all worldly engagements, whether Nazi or non-
Nazi, are to be 'as if not'. But Nazi commitment is not like socialist or
liberal commitment in that it is perfectly possible to be, say, an SPD
member as if one were not, but not to be a Nazi as if not. Idolatry here
acquires a meaning quite intelligible in 'secular' terms: that one's engagement in the world becomes entanglement in the world. All kinds of
engagement in the world can become entanglements. But some kinds can
only exist as entanglements, and these are incompatible with authenticity.
The concepts of engagement and entanglement here correspond to
Heidegger's 'Being-in-the-World' and 'falling'. It has often been noted that
Heidegger is re-working a religious notion here: the Augustinian notion of
sin as turning from the Creator to the creatures; in Heidegger, from Being
to beings – which in *Being and Time* takes the form of fascination with the
entities encountered in the world of our concern rather than choice of our
ownmost potentiality for being (which is in no way that of an isolated atom,
but of Being-in-the-World and Being-with-others). We have here (among
other things) a distinctive stance on the ethics of social institutions: not the
atomist view that they (state, family, associations) are nothing to us but
instruments or obstacles – for they are part of our world and, in a sense, we
are our world; not the idealist concept of 'my station and its duties', which,
while absolutely right as against the atomist, inevitably commits us to idolatry and entanglement; and not *only* the Marxist alternative, 'my station and
its contradictions', which commits us to transforming unsatisfactory institutions into better ones; for even good institutions can be the occasion of
idolatry and entanglement. When Lenin said that from now (1917) on
everyone's politics would be judged by their attitude to the Soviet state, or
when Trotsky adopted the slogan, 'My Party right or wrong', were they not
(in the phrase of another existentialist theologian, Paul Tillich) placing ultimate concern in entities which, however good, are not ultimate? Let me not
be misunderstood: authentic existence is not the business of politics; politics
is essentially concerned with nuts and bolts, with 'soviet power plus electri-
fication', as Lenin put it; I am not criticising the Bolsheviks for lacking a
utopian vision of 'New Socialist Man'. Indeed they were all too prone to
such visions, and 'integral socialism' (as distinct from restrictedly political
and economic socialism) was a part of their downfall. The point is rather
that they should not have placed ultimate concern in politics, and that
having done so, they created entanglements which set the agenda for the
remainder of the history of 'socialism' in the USSR and beyond. Such entanglement is not inherent in Marxism; its *possibility* is inherent in every

institution; its *actuality* is inherent in some other ideologies, such as Nazism. In this last respect, Bultmann got it right.

III

I shall start this section by sketching with the utmost brevity Heidegger's account of conscience, so as to rebut one common charge against it; then I shall look more closely at the notion of *guilt*.

For Heidegger, conscience is a *call*; it is a call of Dasein to itself; it calls *to* Dasein in its everyday absorption with the world of its concern and its lostness in the 'they'; it is the call *of* Dasein's potential authenticity. It does not communicate anything but calls Dasein forth from its entanglements towards its ownmost potentiality for being.

> In calling forth to something, the 'whence' of the calling is the 'whither' to which we are called back.
>
> (1967: 325–326)

The potentiality *towards* which it summons Dasein is not any universal ideal, but the concrete potentiality of that Dasein. Such a concrete potentiality can only be 'as Dasein – that is, as concernful Being-in-the-world and Being with Others' (1967: 325). Hence there is no question of its being a call to a solitary life. Nor is it a call to egoism. David Cooper makes a common mistake when he says:

> since an authentic existence ... requires a person to disengage himself from the ways of the 'Public', the 'herd' or the 'they', the remedy for self estrangement is inherently liable to bring him into conflict with his fellows.
>
> (Cooper 1990: 33)

Certainly, the authentic response to the call 'individualises' in one sense of the word. The whence and whither of the call is 'the uncanniness of thrown individualization', the unique, unchosen situation in which the individual is homeless. The call of conscience individualises us in that it takes us out of our refuge in the 'they' and in our entanglement with things, out of all *ponziopilatismo*, and makes us take responsibility for our choice. But that is quite different from making us either selfish or isolated. On the contrary, is it not precisely the pressure of the 'they' that urges egoism on us, just as it is the external pressure of the market that imposes competitiveness on the individual producer. At least in the capitalist world (and that is the world into which Heidegger, like us, was thrown), to succumb to social pressure is to become anti-social; it takes a strong individual stand to 'swim against the stream' and seek the good of others.

Conscience, according to Heidegger, does not give any information, but it does say something: it says 'Guilty!' The so called 'good conscience' which says 'Not guilty' is 'a slave of Pharisaism' (1967: 337) and 'not a conscience-phenomenon at all' (1967: 338). Guilt is ordinarily interpreted as being the cause of a lack in someone else – e.g. if I am guilty of pickpocketing, I am the cause of the lack of a wallet in someone's pocket. Guilt need not however involve law-breaking, or be concerned with possessions; it may also be 'having the responsibility for the Other's becoming endangered in his existence, led astray, or even ruined' (1967: 327). Nevertheless Heidegger sees the ordinary idea of guilt as inadequate in that it belongs to concern with the present-at-hand, and hence with calculations of indebtedness and repayment. He proceeds to formalise the concept of guilt so that these considerations drop out (1967: 328): guilt is defined as '*Being-the-basis of a nullity*' (1967: 329). But in the first place, as 'thrown' into the world, we are never the basis of our own existence. And 'Although it has *not* laid that basis *itself*, it reposes in the weight of it, which is made manifest to it as a burden by Dasein's mood' (1967: 330). We must take over responsibility for our own existence though we did not found it. Furthermore the forward-looking side of our existence, our projection of possibilities, involves choice of *one* possibility out of many. Hence, 'In the structure of thrownness, as in that of projection, there lies essentially a nullity' – so '*Dasein as such is guilty*' (1967: 331).

It seems to me that this presupposes some such ideal of the plenitude of being as Leibniz ascribes to God: the maximum compossibles must be realised, since being as being is good. However, it differs from Leibniz in that the possibilities are not mere logical possibilities, but potentialities of existing beings. Otherwise we would be back with the incoherent notion of maximising being. Admittedly, Heidegger goes on to tell us that it is no use 'taking our orientation from the idea of evil, the *malum* as *privatio boni*' (1967: 332) but his only reason is that these ideas belong to the present-at-hand. While I am quite happy to extend these ideas to the present-at-hand (it too belongs to Being), the concept of evil as the privation of good can be used also of Dasein's being, and that is what Heidegger is tacitly doing; Dasein is essentially guilty because it is inherently unable to realise some of its possibilities, and it is good that all possibilities be realised.

But if we are guilty whatever we do, what should we do? Heidegger's answer is that we should want to have a conscience, i.e. remain open to its call; and that conscience 'calls Dasein *forth* to the possibility of taking over, in existing, even that thrown entity which it is' – hence 'it must only *be* "guilty" *authentically* – "guilty" in the way in which it is' (1967: 333). Since we cannot realise all our possibilities, we must realise that which is most our own, on the basis of our thrown being. Absorption in the world of our concern and domination by the 'they' prevents us from realising that possibility of being which is unique to each Dasein. They lead to an impoverishment of being by closing off original possibilities and reproducing commonplace ones instead. If we are to draw together all the threads of Heidegger's account of authenticity, we must see it, not as self-aggrandisement, but as sacrifice of the everyday self under the domination of the 'they' and of entanglement with the world of our concern, in order that the maximum compossibles be realised. Authenticity is good because the fullness of being is good. As Heidegger says elsewhere:

> The advent of beings lies in the destiny of Being. But for man it is ever a question of finding what is fitting in his essence which corresponds to such destiny; for in accord with this destiny man as ek-sisting has to guard the truth of Being. Man is the shepherd of Being. It is in this direction alone that *Being and Time* is thinking when ecstatic existence is experienced as 'care'.
>
> ('Letter on Humanism', Heidegger 1978: 210)

IV

At this point I am conscious of having neglected one central theme of Heidegger's account of authenticity, namely his account of our being towards death. This is because I think this is one of the weaker points in Heidegger's account, and wrong in important respects. However there is some good in it, and this is compatible with my reading of the concept of authenticity.

The error is encapsulated in the section-heading 'The Seeming Impossibility of Getting Dasein's Being-a-whole into our Grasp Ontologically and Determining its Character'. It is not just a *seeming* impossibility. While I am alive, I am projecting myself upon possibilities which are still outstanding, and so am not a whole. No attitude I may take towards death can alter that – unless perhaps I knew I was to die shortly, and 'settled accounts' with my possibilities. But that is not the situation as Heidegger describes it – he is talking about us all at all times confronting our mortality, even when death is not expected. As Sartre puts it:

> It has often been said that we are in the situation of a condemned man among other condemned men who is ignorant of the day of his execution but who sees each day that his fellow prisoners are being executed. This is not wholly exact. We ought rather to compare ourselves to a man condemned to death who is bravely preparing himself for the ultimate penalty, who is doing everything possible to make a good showing on the scaffold, and who meanwhile is carried off by a flu epidemic.
>
> (1957b: 533)

About this there is nothing one can do since one can 'expect a *particular* death, but not *death*' (1957b: 533).

Nevertheless Heidegger is right that a focus upon our mortality can shake us out of inauthenticity. What is right in Heidegger's discussion of death is best expressed in Dürer's print 'Knight, Death and the Devil'. Death stands by the knight showing him an hour-glass. I take it that he has not come to tell the knight that his time is up, but to warn him that it is finite – the sand in the hour-glass has not run out. The knight looks at once at and past Death, as if to say, 'I know that the future contains my death, but I must ride on into it and fulfil my errand.' There is no turning back: that way the Devil lies in wait. The knight's resoluteness lies in his determination to finish his task, undeterred by Death: in his looking past Death even while facing him.

Notes

Introduction

1 On the proof that you can derive 'ought' from 'is', see Bhaskar's *Scientific Realism and Human Emancipation* (1986) and chapter 6 of my *Critical Realism* (1994); on the intransitive dimension of science see Bhaskar's *A Realist Theory of Science* (1978) and chapter 2 of my *Critical Realism*; on ills as absences see Bhaskar's *Dialectic* (1993) and my review of it, 'The Power of Negative Thinking' (1995).

2 I prefer the term 'worth' to the more familiar 'value', and use it in the title and wherever it does not seem unnatural. As Marx says:

> In English writers of the seventeenth century we still often find the word 'worth' used for use-value and 'value' for exchange-value. This is quite in accordance with the spirit of a language that likes to use a Teutonic word for the actual thing, and a Romance word for its reflection.
>
> (1976, vol.1: 126n)

In some ways I would like to dispense with the word 'value' altogether, since it is so tied up with the idea of *extrinsic* values conferred by us – see also Heidegger's remarks in his 'Letter on Humanism' (in *Basic Writings*, 1978: 228). But I need a concrete noun with a plural for instances of worth, so 'value' will have to do.

1 Are there values independent of humankind?

1 And these are not only the 'neo-pagan' versions; Lovelock himself quotes with approval the following words from a speech by Vaclav Havel: 'If we endanger her [Gaia], she will dispense with us in the interests of a higher value – life itself' (1995: viii).

3 Spinozism: the work of reason

1 In addition to the particular ambiguous response to head/heart dualism, and the stress on the priority of pre-reflective knowledge, I am struck by three other similarities of Macmurray to the continental existentialists: a militant anti-reductionist view of human existence, combined with a somewhat neo-Kantian search for the fundamental concepts necessary (and peculiar) to understanding 'persons' (compare Heidegger's existential analytic); a conception of the personal as defined by an internal negation (compare Sartre's concept of nihilation); and making the overcoming of fear in the face of death central to the existential project (compare all three existentialists on anxiety, and Heidegger on death). In

addition, all four are united negatively by their hostility to bourgeois values and rejection of liberal politics, though this takes such different forms as Kierkegaard's conservative monarchism combined with a retrieval of the values of pre-Constantine patristic Christianity; Heidegger's green fascism; Sartre's libertarian Marxism; and Macmurray's Christian socialism.

2　For instance:

> Scientific thought is spontaneous thought, free thought; and for this very reason it is not merely intellectual. It rests on imagination and tests itself by experiment. It becomes an exciting adventure, demanding faith and courage, risking failure and error and scepticism all the time.
>
> (Macmurray 1932: 82)

3　The sense in which it is true that we are intellectually civilised and emotionally primitive is that we are highly advanced in our knowledge of the mechanical sciences, physics and chemistry, but primitive in our knowledge of each other and our own emotions. But we should not confuse the distinction between intellect and the reason involved in the emotions themselves with the distinction between the mechanical sciences and the knowledge of the human world. Intellect has a role to play in the human world too. Granted, thinking about the human world is not like thinking about the physical world, and when the former tries to imitate the latter's mathematical and experimental methods it leads to disaster. But it is thinking nonetheless.

4　Spinoza's first biographer, the Lutheran minister Colerus, was scandalised that a barber's bill presented after Spinoza's death was made out to 'Mr Spinosa, of blessed memory'. The phrase may have been suggested by his forename Baruch or Benedict, which means 'blessed'.

5　The question of how objects can be causes for Spinoza is a difficult one which I shall discuss in the text. A word here about a preliminary question which those raised in British analytical philosophy in the third quarter of the twentieth century might think serious. It has often been claimed by philosophers out of that stable that the object of a mental state cannot in principle be its cause, because the two are 'logically related'. This can be briefly refuted – indeed over-refuted.

(1) The plausibility of the claim that events that are logically related can't be causally related depends on the idea that if B is logically necessary given A, the contingent relation A caused B can't hold. But when a mental event is caused by its object, there is no necessity involved (other than causal necessity, which is always tendential). The object of a memory might not have caused the memory – it might have been completely forgotten. And the memory-experience, considered phenomenologically as a seeming-memory, could have happened without its object really having occurred. This is rather central to the understanding of intentionality in Brentano's sense. For one thing or event A to be the intentional object of another thing or event B, is precisely for B to be describable only in terms of A, yet for A and B to be ontologically independent, i.e. either could exist without the other. (2) 'The cause of A caused A' is trivial and uninformative, but true, not false or meaningless; (3) in some cases, the most natural and informative way to describe a causing is in terms which make it logically necessary that the effect occurred, given the cause. For instance (to borrow an example from Roy Bhaskar), Tanya closing the door caused the door to be shut; but 'Tanya closed the door' logically entails that the door was shut immediately afterwards. (4) The general point: it is not events themselves that

are logically related, but descriptions of events. Two events may be logically related under one description but not under another.

5 Problems about the worth of being

1 'Confronted with a cancer or a slum the Pantheist can say, "If you could only see it from the divine point of view, you would realise that this also is God." The Christian replies, "Don't talk damned nonsense" '(Lewis 1955: 41).
2 For a more detailed account of this reading of Spinoza, see my 'The Inorganic Body and the Ambiguity of Freedom' (1991a) and (especially) 'The Materiality of Morals: Mind, Body and Interests in Spinoza's *Ethics*' (1991b).
3 Bauthumley does say at the same place that sin is a privative rather than a positive notion (if we read 'privative' for 'primative', as the context seems to require). But this Augustinian aspect goes undeveloped compared with the idea that evil is in the judgement of the beholder.
4 Clarkson does say that he had broken the law in all points except murder, but this is probably an exaggeration. His autobiographical account of his Ranter period was written after his conversion to Muggletonianism, and he is very likely unfair to his earlier belief and practice.
5 This does mean that one use to which Augustine put the idea of the negativity of evil – as an answer to the problem of evil in theodicy – is not helped by it.
6 See Augustine's *On Free Choice of the Will*, book I, ch. 15 on temporal/eternal, and book II, ch. 7 on common/private.
7 See Quine's essay 'On What There Is', in his book *From a Logical Point of View* (1963).
8 See Tillich's *Systematic Theology* (1953, vol. 1: 258): 'The terms "degrees of being", "more being", "less being", are meaningful only if being is not the predicate of an existential judgement but rather if being means "the power of being".' See also his *The Courage to Be* (1962: 173 ff).

6 Away from anthropocentrism

1 Thus Sartre refers to Heidegger's 'abrupt, rather barbaric fashion of cutting Gordian knots rather than trying to untie them' (1957b: 244), and accuses him of solving the problem by definition (of Being-in-the-World). It seems to me wholly appropriate to cut this Gordian knot, i.e. to show from the nature ('definition') of Dasein that the 'problems' of the existence of other minds and the external world do not arise.
2 See the chapter 'Liberation and Instauration' in my book *Socialist Reasoning* (1990) for a fuller account of this.

7 The worth of human beings

1 The term 'metaphysical' has been unfashionable in the twentieth century (and for three centuries before, among empiricists). Heidegger too followed this fashion. But giving metaphysics prissy pseudonyms like 'conceptual analysis' or 'thinking about being' no more avoids it than calling the adulteration of goods 'the sophistication of goods' made dead flies in the currants a healthy addition.
2 The phrase 'having a life to live' seems to me preferable to the fashionable 'self-ownership', particularly since the word 'self' has regrettably ceased to be a reflexive prefix and become a noun. Self-ownership suggests a distance between owner and owned, and might be taken as implying saleability, whereas I read 'having a life to live' as precluding saleability (wage labour).

3 Apologies to W.S. Gilbert for this example (see *The Pirates of Penzance*).
4 I use the term 'communism', not out of any affection for Stalinism or its successors, but because it suggests class politics and the rejection of the market,
   whereas 'socialism' increasingly suggests capitalism with a red nose.

Supplementary essay

1 For those unfamiliar with Heidegger, a note on terminology is required.

Dasein = person or humankind
existentiale (plural **existentialia**) = any fundamental concept required for under-
    standing human existence, corresponding to Kant's categories as the
    fundamental concepts for understanding the objects of empirical knowledge.
thrownness = all that aspect of someone's being of which they are not themselves
    the cause, e.g. one's place and date of birth, sex, race, place in society and so on.
projection = having projects, projecting possibilities, projecting oneself upon one's
    possibilities, i.e. pursuing them. Never used in the psychoanalytical sense.
present-at-hand (or **at-hand**) things considered merely as brute objects –
    contrasted with ready-to-hand (or **to-hand**) things insofar as they are equip-
    ment used by us. Both are also contrasted with Dasein as the three kinds or
    ways of being. (Animals are seen as intermediate between Dasein and the
    present at hand.)
the 'they' = 'Das Man' in German: 'man' is the impersonal pronoun ('one' or more
    colloquially 'they' as in 'they say there's a lot of it about'), 'das' is the neuter
    definite article. The 'they' is the agent of agentless action, the unidentifiable
    authority for public opinion, into which we all disappear evasively much of the
    time.

Bibliography

Aquinas, Thomas *Summa Theologiae* (translation used is from *Introduction to St Thomas Aquinas*, ed. Anton Pegis, New York: The Modern Library, 1945).

Augustine, Aurelius (1961) *Confessions*, trans. R.S. Pine-Coffin, Harmondsworth: Penguin.

—— (1964) *On Free Choice of the Will*, trans. Anna Benjamin and L.H. Hackstaff, New York: Bobbs-Merrill.

—— (1972) *City of God*, trans. Henry Bettenson, Harmondsworth: Penguin.

Benton, Ted (1993) *Natural Relations*, London: Verso.

Bhaskar, Roy (1978) *A Realist Theory of Science*, Hemel Hempstead: Harvester Wheatsheaf.

—— (1986) *Scientific Realism and Human Emancipation*, London: Verso.

—— (1993) *Dialectic*, London: Verso.

Blake, William (1966) *Complete Writings*, London, Oxford University Press.

Bultmann, Rudolf (1964) 'The Task of Theology in the Present Situation', in *Existence and Faith*, London: Collins.

Collier, Andrew (1981) 'Scientific Socialism and the Question of Socialist Values', in J. Mepham and D.-H. Ruben (eds) *Issues in Marxist Philosophy*, vol. 4, Brighton: Harvester Press.

—— (1988) *Scientific Realism and Socialist Thought*, Hemel Hempstead: Harvester Wheatsheaf.

—— (1990) *Socialist Reasoning*, London: Pluto Press.

—— (1991a) 'The Inorganic Body and the Ambiguity of Freedom', *Radical Philosophy* 57: 3–9.

—— (1991b) 'The Materiality of Morals: Mind, Body and Interests in Spinoza's *Ethics*', *Studia Spinozana* 7: 69–93.

—— (1992) 'Marxism and Universalism: Group Interests or a Shared World?', in R. Attfield and B. Wilkins (eds) *International Justice and the Third World*, London: Routledge.

—— (1994) *Critical Realism: An Introduction to Roy Bhaskar's Philosophy*, London: Verso.

—— (1995) 'The Power of Negative Thinking' (review article on Bhaskar's *Dialectic*), *Radical Philosophy* 69.

Cooper, David (1990) *Existentialism*, Oxford: Blackwell.

Dillenberger, John (ed.) (1961) *Martin Luther: Selections from his Writings*, New York: Doubleday Anchor.

Freud, Sigmund (1925) *Collected Papers*, vol. 3, London: Hogarth.

—— (1971) *The Complete Introductory Lectures on Psychoanalysis*, London: Allen and Unwin.

Gilbert, W.S. (1967) *The Savoy Operas*, London, Macmillan.

Heidegger, Martin (1967) *Being and Time*, Oxford: Blackwell.

—— (1978) *Basic Writings*, London: Routledge.

Hessing, Siegfried (ed.) (1977) *Speculum Spinozanum*, London: Routledge.

Kant, Immanuel (1970) *Political Writings*, trans. H.B. Nisbet, ed. H. Reiss, Cambridge: Cambridge University Press.

Kant, Immanuel (1981) *Grounding for the Metaphysics of Morals*, trans. J. Ellington, Indianapolis and Cambridge: Hackett.

Lewis, C.S. (1955) *Mere Christianity*, London: Fontana.

—— (1963) *The Four Loves*, London: Fontana.

—— (1980) *The Last Battle*, London: HarperCollins.

Lovelock, James (1995) *Gaia*, Oxford: Oxford University Press.

MacDiarmid, Hugh (1967) 'A Drunk Man Looks at the Thistle', in *Collected Poems*, New York: Macmillan.

Macmurray, John (1932) *Freedom in the Modern World*, London: Faber and Faber.

—— (1933) *Interpreting the Universe*, London: Faber and Faber.

—— (1935) *Reason and Emotion*, London: Faber and Faber.

Manning, D.J. (1976) *Liberalism*, London: Dent.

Marx, Karl (1968) 'Critique of the Gotha Programme', in *Selected Works in One Volume*, London: Lawrence and Wishart.

—— (1973) *Grundrisse*, Harmondsworth: Penguin.

—— (1976) *Capital*, vol. 1, Harmondsworth: Penguin.

Naess, Arne (1977) 'Spinoza and Ecology', in Siegfried Hessing (ed.) *Speculum Spinozanum*, London: Routledge.

O'Neill, John (1993) *Ecology, Policy and Politics*, London: Routledge.

Plekhanov, Georgi (1974) *Selected Philosophical Works*, vol. I, London: Lawrence and Wishart.

Quine, W.V.O. (1963) *From a Logical Point of View*, New York: Harper and Row.

Ross, Sir David (1954) *Kant's Ethical Theory*, London: Oxford University Press.

Russell, Bertrand (1963) *Political Ideals*, London: Unwin Books.

Sachs, David (1982) 'On Freud's Doctrine of Emotions', in R. Wollheim and J. Hopkins (eds) *Philosophical Essays on Freud*, Cambridge: Cambridge University Press.

Sartre, Jean-Paul (1957a) *The Transcendence of the Ego*, trans. F. Williams and R. Kirkpatrick, New York: Noonday Press.

—— (1957b) *Being and Nothingness*, trans. Hazel Barnes, London: Methuen.

Smith, Nigel (1983) *Ranter Writings,* London: Junction Books.

Soper, Kate (1995) *What is Nature?* Oxford: Blackwell.

Spinoza, Baruch (Benedict) (1985) *Collected Works*, vol. 1, trans. Edwin Curley, Princeton, NJ: Princeton University Press.

Sylvan, Richard (1985) 'A Critique of Deep Ecology', *Radical Philosophy* 40–41: 2–12, 10–21.

Tillich, Paul (1953) *Systematic Theology*, vol. 1, Welwyn: James Nesbit.

—— (1962) *The Courage to Be*, London: Collins.

Timpanaro, Sebastiano (1976) *The Freudian Slip*, trans. Kate Soper, London: New Left Books.

Trotsky, Leon (1964) 'Their Morals and Ours', in *Basic Writings*, ed. Irving Howe, London: Mercury Books.

Woodhouse, A.S.P. (ed.) (1986) *Puritanism and Liberty*, London: Dent.

Zamyatin, Yevgeny (1972) *We*, Harmondsworth: Penguin.

Name Index

Subject Index